Trawling the Century

Jane Brooks

The right of Jane Brooks to be identified as the author of this work has been asserted in accordance with the Copyright, Designs and Patents Act 1988.

Disclaimer:

This work is a memoir of my life. The photographs are mine or from my family and friends. The poetry is my own original work. Lyrics to songs are all by license granted to me by the licensors - full details in the appendix.

ISBN- 9781720096634

With loving thanks to my wonderful family and friends – many of whom have departed this life but all of whom have been with me on my particular life journey and have remained within my heart.

Infinite thanks are due to my daughter – Amanda Brooks – who, through sheer guts and stickability, edited this work, word by word, page by page, and who nagged and bullied me into not only getting on with it but also into deleting useless rubbish. I also thank those of her talented friends who have contributed drawings and photographs to complement the text.

And I applaud my granddaughter Lily. She was, is, absolutely amazing: she researched tirelessly and presented me with a cd she had made, which is a faithful record of Trawling the Century – thank you Lily. True grit. And then she popped off to Uni and achieved a very good degree in Sociology. True grit.

Contents

Lord, is it I . . .?

There is so much good in the worst of us

And so much bad in the best of us

That it behoves not any of us

To talk about the rest of us.

Portrait of the Artist as a Young Man

You 'ave time?

So who reads poetry anyway?
Oh, just the chosen few.
And why is that?
Because it is subjective, or considered so . . .
and because Poetry goes under the general heading of
Hearts and Flowers and that is so not true.

So why write Poetry, for Heaven's sake?
It's not commercial.
It doesn't sell.
And nobody reads it anyway.

Because writers, and that has to include poets,
are driven . . .
And yes, it might be about waves rolling onto the rocks,
or about a pet who has just learned to sit and stay.
Or about war and death . . .
Or, of course, about Love, and for that vast intensity poetry is the most used
vehicle.
Probably.

Or just because something gets you right in the gut . . .
and there is no option.
It has to be set down -
No choice darling!

This compilation is the story of a life, or of several lives.
Mercifully, it is not by any means solely Biographical.
If it gets you in the gut
It only begins in about the Sixties. All work before that was loaned, unwisely, to
the Daughter and as any Parent knows, usually to her cost, lend anything to your
daughter and you will never see it again. Money, never. Jewellery, belts, glitz of
any sort . . . forget it.
Or a folder of work.

'I know exactly where it is Mummy. I'll look it out and let you have it.'
Don't hold your breath.
I mean it.
Yeah right.

Part I

War

So let us set off and step randomly into this journey and see where it takes us. And memory, like life, meanders - as do these pieces . . .

I was just a kid when the Second World War broke out, and when I was 15 my big sister died. Imagine the trauma.

There's a war on and living, as we did, near to Southampton - bombs dropping all over the place . . . the Blackout . . . Rationing . . . restrictions of all kinds - my sister dies.

There was another little sister - aged 3 at the time - but in spite of all the joy she brought, my mother fell ill. Of course she did.

How do you bury your own child . . . and survive?

Olive Lily with Betty Eileen 1923

The war ground on and finally we had V.E. Day - Victory in Europe, followed pretty sharply by V. J. Day - Victory in Japan. The Allies had used the first Atomic bombs and had blasted first Hiroshima and then Nagasaki off the face of the earth. So of course they surrendered. But that doesn't make it right. I can never forget, and nor will others of my age, the terrible images of the result of those bombs when they were shown on the Pathé Gazette news in all cinemas.

So Victory was celebrated and our 'Boys' came home. My brother was one of them. He had served in the R.E.M.E. from 1939 - 1945.

The war was won . . . but there are those who wonder if it were a hollow victory. However, history has proved that mankind had far worse up his sleeve.

And yes, I do know about and grieve over Dresden and other furious bombings . . . and because I am British it makes me complicit. I wish it were not so . . . Moving on . . .

However horrible the war was in the New Forest, just across the channel another part of the family dwelt and tragedy was growing and evolving irrevocably to a quite unthinkable conclusion.

Marjorie was my mother's younger sister. Favourite siblings and best friends. Feisty and spirited youngsters, both fiercely independent, they defended each other at all times and closed ranks against their brothers. They made plans at an early age to leave home as soon as possible and get out into the world. My mother, Olive, didn't get very far. I believe she was quite beautiful and was snapped up at a very young age by a handsome Coldstream Guard on his way out of the First World War.

Marjorie, however, did much better. She managed to get right away and was soon on her way to France. Also very beautiful, she had an added quality - charisma - an attractiveness which I am sure she exploited to the full. Tall and confident, she was an accomplished dancer and soon she found herself part of a Dance Troupe in Paris.

Ah Ha. But in ten minutes a glorious man was after her. And of course they fell in love.

It was a love that was to be tried and tested beyond anything imaginable and somehow it endured.

Gustave was something else. My father was handsome and accomplished but Gustave was suave and elegant. With the looks of a Thirties film star, a quiet charm and a slight hesitance, he quickly won everyone's heart. I loved him at once, but I was only about six or seven when I first set eyes on him . . . and I expect he brought presents.

So this marriage made in Heaven continued . . . and by the time the war broke out in 1939, Marjorie and Gustave had two little boys.

Gustave's work took him travelling and Marjorie spent her time making a beautiful home in Paris, which had become their preferred location, although Gustave's family and their family business were both in Czechoslovakia.

The war brought its own particular brand of horror and torment to this branch of our family. Gustave was Sudeten German and as such had no love for Hitler's Germany, nor had he any intention of taking up arms against places and people he loved. He therefore joined the French Foreign Legion, but ended up in captivity, interned in, I think, a Labour Camp . . . from which he emerged, many years later, a thin shadow of himself, but alive.

Marjorie, as a British citizen, seems to have spent her war in Paris with her boys, beating on the door of the Embassy in desperate attempts to secure her husband's release.

This account of events is not verbatim history, which is fully documented elsewhere, and my reason for recording it is to bring me to the point where the effect of the war, on our intermingled families, became the point at which I started seriously to write. We rejoin the Parisian branch, after the reunion, where another baby had been born . . . one Sylvie-Maria. What an unbelievable relief . . . to be all together again.

In 1945, Marjorie and Gustave made trips to their English family and planned to visit Gustave's Sudeten relatives. After such a protracted absence, they all needed to discuss, again, the family business.

It seems clear that Marjorie had serious misgivings about this journey across Europe, a premonition perhaps, for it is stated in letters to her sisters that she was very fearful and anxious.

Her fear was extreme, all consuming and real. Sadly she said goodbye to her boys, now about 17 and 13, when they made their way reluctantly back to school to England.

In the time before the trip, Marjorie set about making minute arrangements for her children and all the belongings, in the event that she and Gustave should not return. At the very last moment, she took the rings from her fingers and, giving them into the safe keeping of one of her sisters, tearfully said they were to be kept for Sylvie-Maria in the event that she survive and the parents did not. What pathos . . . and how strange.

The day came and the plane took off with Marjorie, Gustave and the baby on board. Unbelievably however, they hit bad weather and the plane crashed on landing. Little Sylvie and one other passenger, who saved her life, were the only survivors. Every one else perished.

Those children lost beloved parents. Olive, my mother, lost her best friend and I lost my glamorous, happy, flapper Aunt.

And after such a terrible and traumatic war.

That was certainly love.

That was certainly war.

'All's fair in love and war'?

You decide . . .

James and Sylvie-Maria

James   Jane   Graham

Dee   Sylvie

Shadow on the Sun

A bright and beautiful day in June. The war was still happening, the family had been up most of the night with a prolonged air raid, but in The New Forest that morning all was well. The mother was singing as she mopped and dusted . . . the smallest girl was watering her little plot of weeds and the big girl was practicing her piano pieces. Ever watchful, the mother stepped out into the garden. Listening, she quickly gathered up the smallest girl and called urgently to the big one. They stood, this odd trio, simply looking up into a blue and cloudless sky as two or three big mosquitoes came into sight from the north. These were at once followed by more . . . and more . . . and more.

Soon the entire sky was filled with these black creatures and a shadow formed over the sun. The mother saw no immediate danger and so they watched. 'Buzz,' said the smallest girl, pointing a fat little finger skyward. 'Bzzzz . . . Bzzz . . . Look.' As they watched, the swarm came closer and into focus. They were not mosquitoes at all, they were small balsa wood gliders, exactly like the kits that were given away free with Quaker oats, each one pulled by a thin strand of cotton.

The smallest girl clapped, then picking up her little painted tin watering can, she tottered off, to get on with the job in hand.

The sound of the engines of the planes towing the gliders, became loud and whirring, the cotton strands became cables and the sky disappeared in this mass of low flying aircraft.

Mother and daughter watched for a long time, until finally it was over. The sky was blue again. All was normal again.

But as the mother turned to go into the house, wringing her hands, she said quietly 'All those boys . . .'

* * *

The war took me into my teens. I can't say that to begin with I was much affected by it all. The rationing was a bit tedious . . . but, like everyone else in the village, my father dug up our considerable garden and planted vegetables. Cooking had always been my mother's strong point and life went on. By autumn 1940 however, it all hotted up. Rationing, the Blackout and shortages of all kinds started to become more noticeable. And my education was altered. I minded that. A lot.

Southampton was only ten miles away and sirens, searchlights and flak were nightly visitors. One day in particular was more than significant. A German plane came in over Bournemouth, low flying, and machine gunned all along the A31 nearly into Winchester, a distance of about 50 miles. One person was killed and that is to be regretted . . . but at about 5 o'clock on a week day afternoon, the number could have been in the thousands.

Aged just 12, I had been sent to the farm over the road to pick up the eggs . . . and that fact started a chain reaction which averted disaster for our family in particular. My new baby sister, Rachel, had been born only a week before which makes this episode the end of September 1940.

Because of nightly Air Raids, everyone was sleeping downstairs on makeshift beds. Holding her precious baby, my mother had made her way into the kitchen and was sitting by the Range, a grey vitreous enamel Ideal 'Cookanheat'. Not really understanding the terrible noise made by the plane, and fearing for my safety, she went through the hall to look out of the front door. At that moment there was a cracking and searing of glass and the sound of bullets and shattering of wood. The kitchen was in tatters, tea china was broken into bits and flying everywhere and a pewter tea set, complete with milk in the jug and tea in the teapot, was peppered and jagged. The glass in the window was covered in neat round holes - the frame in place and undamaged. My mother and Rachel were saved from almost certain death. That automatic act of 'mother love' had simply moved the chess pieces.

That was a miracle.

Meanwhile I, still over the road, still with my eyes covered by grubby hands, cautiously emerged from the corner of the corrugated iron lean-to where I had taken refuge. The terrible noise had stopped. The plane had continued on its mission of destruction - not that I realised that at the time - but I had peeped between closed fingers and glimpsed the orange tracer bullets.

I watched two teenage girls clamber out of the holly hedge, brushing their skirts and cussing a bit - 'You all right, Rena?' one of them called and they went on their way.

I did the same . . . cussing too. 'Cheek,' I said.

I had been sent for the eggs, so I went on round the wiggly path to the door - and there was the farmer's wife.

'You all right, Rena?' she said.

'Yes fine, thanks,' I said. 'I've come for the eggs.'

I finally got home with the benighted eggs and there was my mother, in a terrible state. 'You all right, Rena?' she cried, clutching me and the tiny baby, somewhat unusually, to her overloaded breast. 'Yes, fine,' I said. 'I've got the eggs.' I couldn't remember when I had had so much attention. And 'What on earth's happened to the stuff on the table?'

Meanwhile my father was travelling home on the top deck of the bus from Southampton. Seeing over the brow of Hunter's Hill he immediately took in what was happening. 'GET DOWN,' he roared. In a war situation the other passengers recognised a voice of authority and dropped like stones.

No one was hit. No one was killed. The bus had been a sitting target. That was another miracle.

I didn't care much for listening to the screaming of the bombs as the crews of damaged aircraft jettisoned their load over the Forest. And then, of course, there were the Doodlebugs and counting the seconds after the engine cut out. Don't ask.

I found the war tedious, puerile and undignified, as you would when you were a kid who knew nothing about the Geneva Convention.

'Jaw - Jaw, not War - War' said Churchill, from his room in the War Office . . . but I think probably Shakespeare got it right. 'The evil that men do lives after them . . .'

And it was following all of that, culminating specifically in the Plane Crash, that I felt compelled to 'write it down.'

However, although those years are deeply embedded in my psyche, all that early work is lost . . . which, upon reflection, is probably just as well, since it would almost certainly have been an earnest, youthful rant against God, the world and everything . . . and best laid to rest.

It did, though, set my style - the genre in which I would work. Uncertainty? Anxiety? Justice? Hope and always Love.

Paddy

26 June 1928 - 16 September 2008

'My name is Paddy,' the voice said. 'Paddy Gallahawk.'

What a fantastic name. A bit of a mouthful but I was very impressed and I rather hesitated to say, 'and I'm Rena . . . Rena Bennett.' It sounded a sort of non name. I was a new girl and she had been assigned to show me around. We were both about 12.

I looked at this girl and the first thing I noticed was how pretty she was. She had lovely hazel eyes and beautiful Shirley Temple curls, which were obviously natural and there on a full time basis, I mean.

I thought of the agonies I suffered every night, sleeping with my hair wound up in rags just to get some semblance of a bend in it . . . and here she was . . . I think I started to hate her there and then!

'Come on,' she said. 'I'll show you where to put your stuff. Oh and the loo's in there and here is our classroom.' She put her things on one of the desks. 'You can sit there,' she said. That was my initiation into Granville College.

When the war had started, the school had been evacuated from Southampton and Paddy was a weekly boarder. We were an unlikely pair . . . she quiet and gentle and I, well, not. But somehow we became firm friends and it was a friendship which was to endure for nearly 70 years.

In 1940 Southampton docks were a prime target . . . the city was burnt out . . . and even the New Forest took a fair smattering of bombs when damaged planes jettisoned their load. Troops were camped in the forest and the main roads were alive with huge convoys of tanks and troop carriers. Parents were at pains to impress upon us to 'be careful and keep your wits about you.'

But it was not all bad.

Those were the days of the silver screen and Paddy and I had our fill. She, incidentally, decided she really couldn't stand being a boarder and, with some misgivings on her parents' part, was allowed to go home and travel daily to school on the bus. I picked up the same bus as it went through my village.

School was what it was. The war raged around us . . . and it really did. Quite honestly, I don't believe we understood the enormity of all that was going on. We were just kids and of course we simply got on with it. It was only later we were to understand the real Political, Economic and Social implications.

Southampton was a working port so of course it was interesting to the 'Enemy'. Most evenings and throughout the night German planes droned over us, the sound of their engines quite unmistakable. A regular pulsing, which I suppose, must have been a feature of their design.

We had complete shut down on light and from just before 'lighting up time' until well after dawn, we existed in an inky blackness which seemed to encompass our world and permeate the house both inside and out.

So that was the 'Black Out' - and then there was Rationing. It is only with hindsight that I can begin to imagine how our parents coped. Everyone in the land was issued with a Ration Book and with the minute amounts of butter, marg, lard, tea, sugar and meat our mothers magicked up full scale meals. It generated in us all a complete 'No Waste' policy, a rule which most people of our generation abide by today.

Of course to us then, it did not really signify . . . the no sweets, no biscuits, no fruit regime was rather boring but Paddy and I soon got it sorted. Either you bought a small amount of something you couldn't live without, or you bought a vast amount of liquorice (with obvious results) plus millions of dolly mixtures, and somehow mixed the two . . . oh, it was all quite disgusting. And then of course, there was endless swapping. 'You can have a go on my bike, pony, roller skates for two squares of chocolate and four dabs of sherbet.' Paddy was an only child and far too well behaved to barter . . . but she soon learned.

I had a totally different life. Part of a large family, with an older sister and brother, I soon found ways and means of wheedling around obstacles and being the youngest had certain compensations. In a way I think we envied each other's lifestyles. We seemed to spend most weekends together as well as all the week. Paddy came to us on Saturdays and went home on Sunday afternoons. Ashurst was deemed to be safer than Shirley, which was only a stones throw from Southampton. So we, of course, exploited the situation.

So imagine . . . Southampton was blessed with dozens of cinemas and we saw everything. All the Golden Oldies in black and white, you name it, we saw it. The air raid warning (the siren) sounded often, just when it got to the good bit, (a notice was flashed up on the screen informing the groaning audience of this fact) but we soon got blasé and just sat tight. I swear the man on the projector turned up the volume and Betty Grable or Sabu resumed and peace was restored. Then we went back to Paddy's for tea before returning to my house. If we were clever and timed it right, we managed to swan in, say a couple of words to the parents, then quickly catch the next bus to Lyndhurst, to another pretty awful flea pit and start the process all over again.

Our mothers were brighter than we gave them credit for and I can't say we got away with that one very often. Even in those dark days of war, the phones still worked.

I loved Paddy's house. It was in a quiet road but it was in the TOWN. I remember a large double fronted stone house. The paved front garden had shrubs and rose beds and a wide front step. Inside, the hall seemed big and each side, symmetrically, was a door. Through the right hand door you stepped straight into Wonderland. A large bow window dominated and light flooded in. There were gorgeous antiques all around . . . glazed cabinets displaying exquisite pieces of porcelain and fine silver, highly polished furniture of inlaid mahogany, delightful small chairs dotted around and pretty Georgian wine tables. Bookcases housing leather bound volumes, family photographs and trinkets . . . and there, centrally to all of this, in a high backed wing chair, sat a tiny little lady, beautiful white hair piled on the top of her head. This was Paddy's Grandmother.

Now it was my turn to be polite and awed. I did both with sincerity. I saw Grandma often after that and soon grew to love and respect her. The room on the left of the front door was probably her bedroom. I never saw that or a Grandfather . . . and of course, I never asked. Beyond the hall and wide oak stairs, spread a large, warm, welcoming kitchen, where Mrs Gallahawk dwelt.

15

By the time I arrived she was usually dishing up a steaming lunch which she, like my mother, seemed to produce out of nothing. Mr Gallahawk carved and lunch was served. He was a retired Merchant seaman . . . a jolly man full of quips, jokes, and discipline. I loved them both and mercifully they seemed to like me. This then, was the pattern of our lives.

And so back to school.

Life wasn't all high jinks and we did work hard. There is no doubt at all that our education was hampered by the restrictions of war. Lack of staff was probably where it was most in evidence . . . long retired teachers, well into their dotage, staggered along to fill the breach. It was funny but hardly productive. We did start a Guide troop in which Paddy really shone and indeed she stayed in the movement for many years as a Guider. She loved dancing . . . ballroom and Greek on Friday afternoons . . . as much as I hated it . . . 'for Heaven's sake Rena, move. I'll have to be the man again, I suppose. Now, one two three and back.' Oh please NO. Dance I could not. But run I could, and play a mean game of tennis and sing, a bit.

But time moves on and we were in the 6th form when we both left Granville to start all over again elsewhere. We lost touch for a while, sowing our wild oats, making inappropriate marriages, having babies . . . all those things and changing our names of course, which didn't help.

But we did catch up.

My mother had found her mother in the phone book. No mistaking that name. And it was great. And joyous. And just the same, of course. Paddy's kids were about 10 and 3 and mine about 4 and 2. Something like that. We kept in touch through all the good times and all the traumas and the constant hard graft, and somewhere in the seventies, when we were both free to see each other more often, we did. We spent some holidays together between having our hearts broken on several more occasions and we grew old by phone . . . she in Hampshire where she had made a good life, and I happily settled in Dorset.

On the 16th of September 2008, Paddy died. I miss her so much. The end of a life time friendship.

She quiet and gentle . . . and I, well, not.

In my life . . .

There are places I'll remember all my life
though some have changed,
some forever, not for better,
some have gone and some remain.
All these places had their moments,
with lovers and friends, I still can recall,
some are dead and some are living,
in my life I've loved them all.

Though I know I'll never lose affection
for people and things that went before,
I know I'll often stop and think about them.
In my life, I love you more . . .

Lennon & McCartney 1965

But I hadn't been the youngest forever and Rachel had come along, not with a whimper but with a bang.

In September 1940, at the very height of all that was unholy, she had made her gentle appearance.

Bombs blasting over Southampton, desperately trying to annihilate the docks and all that lay en route. Trees in the forest being torn up by their roots . . . mighty oaks which had been around for three hundred years, some more, having themselves witnessed wars and disasters before, though never of such intensity, stood proudly shaking off the litter of planes and bodies and shrapnel as it landed upon and around them. 'Stand firm,' rustled the most senior of them all, the Knightwood Oak, then over 400 years old. That tree survived throughout my earlier life and may be there still, cosseted as it was and always had been, just within striking distance of the Rufus Stone.

And so it was into this mayhem that Rachel had emerged. Her cot was in the side room, the ersatz air raid shelter, and there she received a constant stream of my friends, which was allowed 'as long as they were clean and didn't get too close.'

It was soon after this event, when she was only a few months old, that Gas Masks were issued to everyone in the land, including babies. There was intelligence of possible Gas attacks from the air, which mercifully never materialised, but Britain stepped up to the mark.

I didn't mind too much about the look of these masks, but Paddy, always more aware of appearances than I, minded a lot. These masks came in very strong square cardboard boxes with a shoulder carrying cord. Inside every box were 'Instructions for Use in the Event of an Enemy Attack and 'To be Carried At All Times.' We had regular practice runs at school and at home, when our fathers told us to 'take it seriously . . . it might save your life one day.' So we all cavorted about looking like Mickey Mouse, seeing no danger and viewing the whole thing with derision.

Rachel's mask, however, was a far more complicated and serious affair. It was like a little enclosed carrycot. The top was a transparent window made I think of mica (the precursor of plastic), and into this contraption the baby was placed - in this case Rachel. She seemed relatively happy and obliged by clenching her tiny fists and wiggling her tiny feet. My mother cried, my father comforted her by saying 'It will probably never happen, my dear,' and I believe I was rather chastened by the whole episode.

Mercifully, my father was right. The Gas Attack never came.

Olive Lily Bennett with Rachel Helena c. 1952

William Harold Bennett . . . JOE

1880 - 1953

My father was the second son of seven children born to a Victorian family in Winchester, Hants. That is a very long time ago and I knew little of those children and really nothing of my Grandparents.

There were various maiden Aunts who all seemed to move in with us separately and severally, and who brought with them different attributes. Through them the linen was kept in a state and many are the miles of sheets which were sewn 'sides to middle' and many were the pairs of socks darned into obscurity. Others of them excelled in washing and ironing fine linen, so our table was always laid with lovely cloths and napkins. One was particularly 'good with the children' and suffered us, at varying stages of our growth, to crawl all over her. Another named 'Tot' had her silky white hair piled atop her head and secured with a small black velvet bow. She had periods of being slightly batty and was sent off to 'take the waters' but when she was functioning on all four cylinders, she was truly a mine of information. She spent hours telling us stories, reading us endless books and reciting reams of poetry and verse. She was a good sort and was the last to depart this world in, I think, the early forties.

Joe grew tall and strong, a quiet, thoughtful and gentle boy, and when faced with the choice of Church or Army, he chose the latter. He, too, was full of tales. Apparently he rode a 'Penny Farthing' bicycle and was the first to ride from Winchester to Southampton on a bike with pneumatic tyres. Looking back some time later, at what and how little I have written about my father, I found myself sad. Is that little bit of trivia really the sum total of my knowledge of him? I realised that his life was in two distinct halves. And really I knew only the second half.

He would have been 45 years old when I was born and, bearing in mind I had two older siblings, he must have been 40 when he came out of the Guards. Whether he had served his time or was invalided out I do not know and there are no contemporaries around to fill me in. They too, would be 130 plus now.

So all that I know of his youth is hearsay - and probably skimmed over by him and glamorised by his adoring sisters, all those maiden aunts who came to stay, or who lived with us and did miles of stitching.

The bit we heard from him of his time in the Service was portrayed as insignificant, amounting to nothing, even though we knew he respected that time. He spoke only of the pranks, not the time in action and almost never of the hideous time in the mud and carnage of the trenches in the Great War 1914 - 1918. Only when we saw his wounds did we have a glimpse of the horror. It was all well guarded - perhaps too painful in terms of men lost - perhaps even then an embryonic Official Secrets Act. I cannot know.

But that was then and this was now and as far as WHB was concerned, the Peace proved every bit as gruelling as the War.

Launched back into an entirely different Great Britain from the gay and carefree time of his youth, he and the depleted thousands of returning troops arrived to a post war period of poverty, depression and unemployment.

Probably entirely unqualified, having come straight from school, these boys had to buckle down and get on with it. By 1920/21 or 2, married and soon to have a young family to support, Joe was no different from the rest. The freedom, the privilege and the gentility, really, of his upbringing and early life, had been swept away by 'the war to end all wars' . . . Joe, like all his compatriots, had to face up. And perhaps none the worse for all that. Grasping the nettle can only ever be good.

He coped, of course. He grew in spite of, or probably because of, the War, into a responsible member of the then society, a loving husband and a caring father.

He was a good man.

Sadly, there are no photographs, even snaps. Money would have been short. Cameras expensive and developing - extortionate. A needless luxury. Or perhaps he was taking, and rationing, the few tiny black and white images that appear of that time. I have searched long forgotten folders of 'stuff' and asked around but have turned up nothing - except the hideous one or two, still black and white, of my wedding, in 1949.

Joe and Olive Lily   Rena Jane and Joe

'We don't visit, we rarely entertain and when invited, wherever possible, we decline.'
WHB

The Soldier

If I should die . . . think only this of me;
That there's some corner of a foreign field
That is forever England. There shall be
In that rich earth - a richer dust concealed;
A dust whom England bore, shaped, made aware,
Gave once, her flowers to love, her ways to roam,
A body of England's, breathing English air,
Washed by her rivers, blest by suns of home.

And think . . . this heart, all evil shed away,
A pulse in the eternal mind, no less
Gives somewhere back the thoughts by England given;
Her sights and sounds; dreams happy as her day;
And laughter, learned of friends - and gentleness,
In hearts at peace, under an English heaven.
Rupert Brooke 1887 - 1915

Rupert Brooke was a fellow of King's College, Cambridge, when the Great War broke out. Initially ill disposed towards the war, his mood changed and he patriotically enlisted.

Joining the Royal Naval Division, he saw service at Antwerp in 1914, but died of blood poisoning on his way to Gallipoli, in April 1915.

And . . . Reconciliation . . .

When you are standing at your hero's grave,
Or near some homeless village where he died
Remember, through your heart's rekindling pride
The German soldiers who were loyal and brave.

Men fought like brutes; and hideous thing were done;
And you have nourished hatred, harsh and blind.
But in that Golgotha perhaps you'll find
The mothers of the men who killed your son.

Siegfried Sasson 1886 – 1967

And just around the corner was another War, even more horrendous than the last.

Peace is Good

When the noise stops
and the lights go on -
and the boys come home,
with both their legs
or not -

When Mothers finally dry their tears
and Fathers stop pacing -
and being cross
and the kids feel safe again -

When the men in the House
stop huffing and puffing - and say, quite simply
'We must do better' . . . and mean it.

When all is quiet and the dust has settled
And the men in the Church say
Let us pray

Peace is Good

D. Day 6th June 1944 – 65 years on

The whole country is thinking about D. Day. Today is 6th June 2009 and I feel pretty cross and so, I'm sure, will a lot of other people. The thing that sticks in my veteran mind is that it has turned into a multi-cultural Political cock up. This could well be the final D Day celebration for many or most of the serving Forces, individuals who were there . . . present on those beaches.

Her Majesty the Queen was not invited to attend.

The Queen, then Princess Elizabeth, was serving in the war at that time. She was there and those veterans wanted their Sovereign with them on this, possibly their last, D. Day gathering. In the event, the ceremony was attended by Prince Charles and by the Prime Minister, Gordon Brown . . . and although I have a great deal of time for both of them, neither had been there. The Queen had been. Shame on them.

* * *

Paddy and I were there, in somewhat less noteworthy circumstances it is true . . . but nonetheless there. We were about 15 at the time and we were at school, in Lyndhurst, in the New Forest. It was timetabled that the Upper School gathered in the hall every Friday morning, where we listened and took part in the Service for schools, on the wireless. June 6th 1944 was different.

The announcer said, 'This is the BBC Home Service and here is the News and this is Alvar Liddell reading it. The service for schools will not be broadcast today. We are bringing you news of an important development in the war,' he went on. 'Today the British Expeditionary Force has landed on the beaches in France . . .' and he went on to report exactly what was happening, as we listened.

After a while the Head asked if we wanted to continue to listen or to 'file quietly back to your classrooms and continue with your lessons.' To be honest the announcement was mostly repetitious and fairly boring, once we got the main gist. (We might have become a bit Gung Ho about the war, which we perceived as a curb on everything,) but faced with the choice of listening or double maths, there was no contest and of course we sat there. It was only after I got home and my father was listening attentively, that the whole thing was put into perspective.

And now Henry Allingham and Harry Patch, 'The last Tommy,' have both recently died. Both were in the First World War. At his funeral service in Wells Cathedral on 6th August, Harry Patch was quoted as saying, 'Compromise not Confict.' I agree of course . . .

'Beware you win the War and lose the Peace'

All that is needed for Evil to flourish . . . is that Good Men do nothing . . .

* * *

We Can Work it Out

Try to see it my way . . .
Do I have to keep on talking till I can't go on?
While you see it your way,
Run the risk of knowing that our love may soon be gone
We can work it out.
We can work it out.

Think of what you're saying
You can get it wrong and still you think that it's all right.
Think of what I'm saying,
We can work it out and get it straight,
Or say goodnight.
We can work it out.
We can work it out.

Life is very short
and there's no time for fussing and fighting my friend.
I have always thought that it's a crime,
so I will ask you once again

Try to see it my way,
Only time will tell if I am right or I am wrong,
While you see it your way,
There's a chance that we may fall apart before too long.
We can work it out.
We can work it out.

Life is very short
and there's no time for fussing and fighting, my friend.
I have always thought that it's a crime
so I will ask you once again

Try to see it my way,
Only time will tell if I am right or I am wrong,
While you see it your way,
There's a chance that we may fall apart before too long.

We can work it out!
We can work it out!

Lennon & McCartney 1965

Good, I feel a great deal better now. Thank you Beatles . . .

Part II

Moving On

1968 - Courthay

It was one of those magical days. Everything was shining, shining and new.

For the very first time she took the key from her pocket and slowly unlocked the door in the old stone wall. She did this with some sort of sense of occasion, for occasion it certainly was. Quietly she pushed at the door and stepped inside. She leaned back until the latch clicked into place. And she just stood there, quite still - quite silent, hardly daring to breathe. She was alone - which is exactly how it should have been. Without moving, she looked around her. It was all as she knew it would be. It was beautiful. It was absolutely beautiful.

She was standing in a garden.

Running along on her left was an old stone house and the garden spread out, along and beyond. Crazy paved paths ran around big beds, filled with tall flowers in bud and in bloom . . . there were shrubs and trees . . . there was an old pergola clad densely with an Albertine, cream buttery buds coexisting happily, jumbled and tangled, with a little white clematis. At the end of the lawn stood an old fir tree, just the sort of tree the kids would want to climb and in the middle, a large, low pendulous flowering cherry, spreading a shower of white blossom like a wedding cake.

But in the long south facing border were poppies . . . a plethora of poppies, with their scarlet paper petals, standing tall, randomly, swaying very gently in an almost imperceptible breeze . . . and their welcome was palpable. It was only then that she moved.

Walking, almost gliding, toward them, on a journey that took a moment or an hour and weeping as she went, she fell on her knees before them, wanting to embrace and thank them. A few had given up a petal or two. These she picked up, very gently, to press in her Bible and slowly and almost with reverence, she walked into the house.

She had come home.

* * *

Settling into the old house was a complete joy. Never afraid of a bit of hard graft the restoration was tackled with gusto.

'Well I like the house Mummy, but I don't like the brown,' was the daughter's reaction at the first viewing . . . so that had to go. Nobody liked it and it went, pronto. White paint quickly covered the brown, walls and ceilings were cleaned and painted . . . there wasn't much furniture and even less money, but it was wonderful. We absolutely loved those weeks, and it was not only the house which was restored.

School continued, homework was tackled and, after all the trauma, life was serene and safe.

But nothing comes free.

With Joy there is frequently a degree of sorrow.

Victory tempered by regret.

Euphoria dampened by the cold hand of reality.

And it was hard.

Divorce is always a tragedy - so said her lovely young solicitor, fresh out of the Fields of Lincoln's Inn, as he steered her through the legal mayhem. He was of course, right.

And no one gets married to get divorced . . . sometimes it is the only solution. The garden was a haven of solace and peace . . . and as she strolled around, plucking at a flower here and pulling at a weed there, she pondered it all.

She thought about Love - her expectations and their ultimate loss. And reasoning with herself, she wrote 'Love is . . .'

Love is . . .

Love is a question
A wondering, doubting, sudden shaft of light
An awareness, small and laughing
Swallowed in the clamour and the noise . . .
A quaint illusion.

Love is a dreading
A frightened shuddering of confused and worried thought –
A nightmare thing to flee from and to cast away
Yet running, comfort and a glow inside.
A shadow in the soul.

Love is a challenge
As unexpected as the sun in winter
and as unpredictable
A boisterous optimist - carefree and capricious
A demon extrovert.

Love is a silent thing
A lonely world of cold interpretation
An agony of conjecture, of weighing thoughts and glances
Of balancing unspoken theories -
The ambiguity of wordless comment.

Love is loyalty
and coming off the fence
An utter single-minded unity of thought and purpose
A willing and entire monopoly -
A star, a two-way oneness.

Love is an arc of music
Incessant calling of a siren violin
A nodding of the flower drums
A movement imperceptible
A rhythm in the bones.

Love is an army, inevitable in its purpose
The trampling, stabbing white hot pain of want
The pulsing, beating throbbing of achievement

The tumultuous ebb and flow of battle joined
The choking mastery of a victory won
A gentle violence.

Love is a quiet thing
The tenderness of sweet acceptance and the peace of giving
Serenity, a contented lull
A compromise, a whispered prayer
The answer.

Moon Days

Taplow 1959

Slowly, silently, now the moon,

Walks the night in her silver shoon,

This way and that, she peers and sees,

Silver fruit upon silver trees . . .

(with apologies to Walter de la Mare if ancient memory misquotes.)

A row of old cars lined the lane opposite the little school. At least they were not old then, some of them were probably new and gleaming . . . Morris Minors, Standard 8s, boxy Fords, Austin 7s and so on and the mothers, the drivers of these super specials, were grouped nervously on the pavement, waiting.

It was 3pm on a sunny September afternoon. We were awaiting our babies, our five year olds, whom we had, much earlier that day, deposited there, with words of encouragement and tears, mostly ours, to dip their unsuspecting toes into the wide sea of Education. The year was 1959.

Younger kids tugged at their mother's hands, jumped about and called excitedly. Most of them hadn't been separated from their siblings ever before. And although there might have been constant battles in the familiar surroundings of home, this was time only for joy and love. Eventually, the little queue emerged and snaked its way towards us across the playground. The band of mothers crossed the lane and stopped at the bottom of the steps. Gradually each little body was swept up into loving arms and triumphantly carried away.

'Simon, Simon,' called the smallie, tugging at my hand . . . and there he was in his blazer and blue cap, long grey socks with the blue flash, oh, and the blue tie, still in place. He came towards us slowly. He looked completely exhausted with a far away look in his eyes. 'Was it all right?' I asked. 'Wonderful,' he said, quietly.

'Have one of these, Si,' said his sister, magnanimously and slightly unusually, offering her bag of sweets.

It wasn't long after this that Simon said in a matter of fact way, 'Mummy, did you know the world is round . . . and also it has a Satterlite? It is the MOON.'

'Well, yes, I did know the world was round actually. Takes a bit of getting used to, doesn't it? And we can go and look at the Satellite right now, if you like.' It was a fine night and the moon was full. 'Let's all go into the garden and see it,' I said. And so we went, the three of us.

It was a wonderful evening, everything was glinting and silver. And there was the moon, shining down on us.

'Strange, isn't it, our Satterlite,' said Simon. 'I must go an' read a bit more about it.' And off he went, his hands behind his back.

Amanda and I stood looking up. I felt a great sense of the enormity of it all and she, my little one, struck a baby ballet position and one arm stretched high into the air, the finger pointing skyward, jetéd prettily and giving a splendid pirouette, announced, 'I'm goin' off to the Sattie Light.'

And there you have it . . . My two adorable kids.

And really, nothing changes.

'Hitch your wagon to a star, old thing,' my father had told me, when I was a little girl.

Amanda needed no such encouragement . . . She had the gene built in. Still has.

A few years passed, during which time we moved to Somerset, leaving behind friends we had all grown to love and trust during those early years in Maidenhead, some of whom are friends still.

Moon Walk

Court Hay - 20th July 1969

Mickey came down from Maidenhead today. He came on his bike, Heaven help us.

Mickey, Amanda (Min) and Simon had been friends when we lived in Maidenhead and he had come for a specific reason. The boys were about 15 and Min a couple of years younger. They settled themselves into the den and prepared for a long night, (complete with Scrumpy, which I knew nothing about, but we were in Somerset after all.)

Without ceremony the television was switched on. Would it have still been black and white in 1969? It wouldn't have mattered anyway, as everything was black and white and fairly hazy.

And there it all was, the moon, the galaxy, the universe . . . Space. Like every other family we sat glued to it. 'We have Lift Off,' shouted Houston.

The world held its breath.

The journey into space.

The crackly commentary from Houston.

Excitement and anxiety was generated by their words and by the conversation and constant checks from the crew in the capsule. And the world waited.

Then the last few (hundred) miles . . . The fantastic views of the moon's surface . . . a weird and ghostly, unreal sort of landscape and finally, touchdown.

The eagle had landed . . . Apollo 11 was down.

We cheered, everyone cheered, the whole world cheered.

The world united in that moment.

We watched, fascinated, as the crew went into work mode and finally Neil Armstrong stepped forth.

And the immortal words . . .

'One small step for man, one giant leap for mankind.'

There has been controversy ever since as to whether Armstrong actually said ' . . . step for a man' or ' . . . step for Man.' I don't care really, he was down. He was taking the very first steps upon an entirely unknown surface, in an entirely, utterly unknown place . . . in Space. Man was walking on the Moon. Eureka!

It was at that point that Amanda and I gave up and the boys got down to the serious business of consuming the scrumpy. Although I hadn't known, I doubt I would have objected if I had. I do remember, however, that both boys looked rather green the next day and Mickey returned to Maidenhead by train.

Or did we take him, by car . . .?

* * *

For Joanie - There has been a sort of sequel from Simon.

I had sent these pieces to Simon and asked him on the phone if he had read them. Simon is always at the airport when we speak, so the conversations are pretty brief, but on this day he seemed almost interested. And he filled in lots of bits I either didn't know or had forgotten. Oh yes, he remembered it well. Mickey had brought a friend with him, couldn't remember friend's name, and they HAD come on bikes. He said they had all gone off and bought a gallon, that's A Gallon, of Scrumpy. They hid that well.

He said that Min and I had gone off to bed as soon as Apollo had landed. Min was only about 12 and I was obviously shattered. However, I had apparently asked them to call me before the Walk. I knew I had seen the First Steps but hadn't remembered the interim.

I did not, however, see any signs of booze. I wouldn't have been looking for them of course. Apparently, the interim period was 5 hours. It gets better. Simon started to laugh, remembering it all. 'We put away so much drink,' he said. 'At least, Mickey did.' Good old Mick, nothing changes.

Simon quite warmed to his subject and between the giggles he said, 'Mickey went to sleep on the loo. He did, he went to sleep . . . on the loo. He sat there, on the loo, holding on to a towel rail or something . . . and he was asleep . . . out cold.'

I believe Simon was rather impressed, probably still is. So am I. Good old Mick.

I like this bit of the story. The bits you don't know about your kids are often the funniest.

Because . . .

Because the world is round it turns me on

Love is all, Love is you.

Because the wind is high it blows my mind,

Love is old, love is new.

Because the sky is blue it makes me cry

Love is all, love is you.

Lennon & McCartney 1969

Plus ça change . . .

So Simon's all growed up now. All over the years he has continued to make me proud.

During his Gap Year he got a job as a waiter in an hotel in Devon. With part of his first salary, he bought me a pair of porcelain figures, which he gave me on my birthday that August. He will have forgotten . . . I have not and of course I have them still.

The thing he will probably remember about this episode was that all the studying that he was doing went up in smoke. One of his fellow slaves fell asleep on the floor, while smoking. The bedroom in the staff house and most of the contents went in the ensuing blaze. Simon was not best pleased but both boys were all right. Anyway, at Oxford he read PPE at Queen's and then Economics at Nuffield. By this time his interest in economics had clearly emerged.

SJB – middle, back row.

From there he went for six years directly into The National Institute for Social and Economic Research, where he wrote a tome with a couple of colleagues, called The Exchange Rate Environment. I have of course read the Forward and quite a lot of the Introduction, until I lost the will to live, the main body of the book being written in a foreign language. (English, of course, but not the sort of English of which I have any knowledge and which is therefore entirely beyond me.)

The book, over 30 years old now, still sits proudly on the bookcase.

From The Institute, Simon did a twenty year stint at the Treasury, for which he received a CB – Companion of The Order of The Bath. We all went to The Palace to witness this momentous occasion. I seem to remember Simon groaned a lot but he did give us lunch in Smith Square, which was good. Alas, the chance of a second visit to the Palace by a proud mum to witness something even better has now passed - so we shall not be calling him Sir.

He went on to work for the European Investment Bank and was based mainly in Luxembourg. We spoke regularly on the phone but even as I write this I can feel him cringing as he corrects all the stuff I've got wrong. So I shall stop.

However, he likes to run, to cycle, to play tennis and especially, on the rare occasions that he brings his family home, he likes to walk the beautiful Dorset coast.

So I did write a piece for him about the Dog Walk. It is called 'Hope.'

He might have read it . . . and groaned. I'm not sure.

Hope . . . the other option

1st August 1993 For Simon

But then . . .
at the end of the day
when all is said and done
at the end of the lane
past the BunHausen row
with their scarecrow heads
and Albertine wigs,
mellow in the low-glow, sun-glow day. . .
Dance on.

Dance past the paddock . . .
where in the bright of the swaying grassy floor,
a Piebald and a Palamino
enquire, nodding, of your kindness and your pocket.
Dance on.

Dance past the tents and the small green moving homes,
squatting in their tidy urban rows,
where in their topsy-turvy roles,
fathers turn the spitting pan
upon reluctant flame
and mothers, languid, sip their Pimms . . .
Dance on.

Dance youthful, joyful, over the stile
and into the golden corn.
Look at it . . . but see it
Touch it . . . but feel it
Know it.
It holds for you a promise
It is the staff of life.
Dance on.

Dance up the winding,
fast up the winding,
throw up your arms in the clamour
of the gull-laden, scent-laden day . . .
Breathe deep, gasp, choke if you must
only live it - - - the blueness - - - the wonder.
Dance on.
Dance on. You are nearly there. Dance on.

You should stop now. Be still.
For you are come.
Place your hot hands over your eager eyes
and pray the gift of sight.
Now you may look. Look now.
Drink in the sea . . .
The Kingdom, the Power and the Glory . . .
For it is there. It is everywhere.
The measure of the smallness of all things.
And you have found it.
At the end of the lane. . .
At the end of the day.
Dance on.

The Bunhausen Row

Mellow in the low - glow, sun - glow day . . .

The Blueness, the wonder . . .

Simon Brooks appointed

Vice-President of the EIB

Release date 27 July 2006

Simon Brooks, a former Director in the Macroeconomic Policy and International Finance Directorate of the UK Treasury, has joined the European Investment Bank (EIB) as Vice-President. He has been appointed as the British member of the EIB's Management Committee, to succeed Peter Sedgwick. As a member of the Management Committee, Simon Brooks becomes part of a team of 9 - the President and 8 Vice-Presidents - who are appointed by the Bank's Board of Governors (the 25 Ministers of Finance of the EU member Countries).

Simon BROOKS, CB
EIB Vice-President

As the Bank's permanent executive board, the Management Committee, under the leadership of the President and the supervision of the Board of Directors, runs the Bank in line with the missions assigned by the Board of Governors. Once appointed, the Vice Presidents are responsible solely to the Bank. Simon Brooks started his career at the National Institute for Economic and Social Research in London. He joined the UK Treasury in 1985 as an Economic Advisor, working initially on

macroeconomic analysis of the UK, and subsequently as a member of the Monetary Group on monetary policy, EMU, Maastricht and other monetary issues. In 1992, he became Head of Division, Economic Analysis Group (EA), responsible for analysis and forecasting of the UK economy. From 1994 until 1998, he was Head of the Regional and Country Analysis team, working on overseas economies and their impacts on the UK, and also on a number of international economic issues such as, for example, globalisation, the implications of ageing, world saving and investment, and capital liberalisation. From 1998 to 2000, he was Head of EU Finance, working on the UK's financial relationship with the EU and on Agenda 2000. He then became Director of Macroeconomics with broad responsibilities, including, for example, UK and world economic forecasts, and fiscal and monetary policy frameworks.

Mr Brooks gained a masters degree in economics from the University of Oxford in 1978, following his undergraduate studies - also at Oxford University - in politics, philosophy and economics. Mr Brooks took up his post on 1 July. He can be contacted at the Headquarters of the EIB in Luxembourg, where he is now resident.

Founded in 1958 by the Treaty of Rome, the European Investment Bank, the EU's long term financing arm, is the world's leading multilateral development institution in terms of the volume of financing provided (47.4 billion in 2005). It is also the foremost non-sovereign borrower on the capital markets, raising some EUR 50 billion a year. Its lending operations focus on both modernising the economies of the Member States of the European Union and fostering the development of countries outside the EU.

'The ears have re-emerged, I am afraid, as the hair has thinned back to the quantity in the previous photo . . .' to quote Si.

Part III

The Dream Sequence

I have spread my dreams

Under your feet.

Tread softly,

because you tread on my dreams.

W.B. Yeats 1865 – 1939

Poets are inveterate dreamers. Goes with the territory, I'm afraid. No doubt this facet can be tedious for proper people . . . but where would we be without our dreams. It seems to me that Dreams, like Hope, are an entirely essential part of the persona. How else would the washing up ever get done? Waking or sleeping, our dreams, our visions, and our imagination go along with us.

Step outside and taste the air after rain,
Try to see beyond the city smoke.
See the colours as they really are.
Listen to the river, the breeze caught in the trees.
Feel the weather on your skin.
Stand small amidst the mountains,
watch flowers and grasses tremble and sway
Observe through warm eyes. . .
tread carefully, guardian of creation,
we were only given one world.

Author unknown

Dream Walking

In the moment of my waking you were there.

And you were beautiful.

We were young again and in your love you came to surprise me.

And so you did. I was as I was - my face washed shiny and an old blue bath hat on my head.

Why had you not warned me . . . so I could paint upon my face a picture and braid my hair?

But there we were.

You arrived in a huge black car, open at the top, and left it there at the door, while you knocked.

The school Matron, who was Rosemary, let you in.

She was as she always is, large - hair straight - and behind her glasses her kind, eyes smiling.

Hand in hand we went.

The stairs curved away in a spiral. An Elizabethan house with the stairway thrown on outer as an after thought.

We ran together down a long, long corridor and out into the sunshine.

And there, in the wonderful open car, sat five dirty children - their eyes shining in their filthy faces. They were clapping and shouting.

We did not mind. You threw them some pennies and they were gone.

I don't remember driving in the glorious black car, for there in the sky above us, a big old monoplane, white with red markings, flew low and spluttering.

As we watched, one wing simply folded down, like the arm of a signal   on a railway line.

Powerless and transfixed we watched in silent horror as the whole thing just fell out of the sky . . . out of sight.

An orange mushroom filled everything, a sickening roar and a puffing of enormous sound.

Somehow we burst into life.

We knew that the plane had fallen into an urban area and that in the middle was a school.

We were in a 'phone box choking out our message.

Then everything was changed.

We were staggering up a flight of unfriendly concrete steps which gave onto a vast car park. A red brick wall followed the lie of the steps and when we reached the top our time had run out.

You leaned back against the wall and crumpled slowly down. Is that all there is?' you said.

I bent to take you in my arms but in the bending I awoke.

And you, of course, were gone.

You have been gone these many years, but I was smiling as I woke

You loved me then.

49

Just Passing Through

He stepped into my dream last night.
A shimmering radiance, entirely recognisable,
essentially the same. Glowing with universal love
and displaying some kind of deep knowledge.
Then he was gone.
Evidently just passing through.

Seventy today, he would have been.
They had been planning a party, something spectacular
and a huge cake, with thousands of candles.
And chatter. . .
And people, carefully chosen
in dinner suits. . . slightly shiny
and posh glittery frocks,
preserved from the eighties.
And all their grown up seedlings
popping corks all over the place
and passing quail eggs.

And she slightly apart . . .
Glowing quiet in white and pride
and he, in the middle of everyone
of everything . . .
shooting off party poppers, like billiho,
covering all in clouds of neon streamers,
droplets of generosity, touching everyone,
like wax from the candles, never lit . . .
and the rockets, never quite set off for Mars.

And her response

I will be there as I promised
I will wear my Sunday Best.
You will know me when you see me
With your rosebuds at my breast . . .
On my sleeve a heart is glowing,
In my eyes will be the stars . . .
I will be there as I promised,
I will meet you under Mars.

Paul Smyth 9.12.02

Mary - For Paul

How is your beauty told
How tell the golden thread
Gently entwining love and quiet faith -
Which is your beauty.

How tell the laugh, the voice,
The eyes, the smile, the glorious hair . . .
How tell the glowing face.
The playful eyes, purring and provocative,
Timeless in perception
Generous in compassion
Transparent to the essence.

The mouth, pursed in anxiety,
Yet full in pride of gathered brood,
Aware consuming human love
Itself Divine.

And the hair, shaming Rossetti,
Now framing the Madonna
Now shepherdess
All threaded strands.

The face of serenity,
Of ageless pathos -
stolen by time,
Yet now and Hardyesque
Giving the bubbly joy of love
Unquestioned and expansive.

Here is a thread of abstracts.
Why fragment the mystery
And so diminish it.
How tell the golden thread
How tell your beauty?

Dr and Mrs Paul Smyth
'enough is too much!'

Requiem

'She is doing so well. She is looking better.'
Thus we excuse our pathetic inadequacy.
'She is getting there. She is looking stronger.'
Thus we insult her courageous exposure
to world she wants no part of . . .
wishing to go nowhere . . . say nothing . . . see no one.

She is learning to say, 'The day he died'
rather than, as before . . .
'That day, that dreadful day.'
That day will never change, but aware,
she spares the discomfort of others.

He had asked her sweetly, not to forego the niceties
and so she carries . . . every evening . . .
a pillar and tripod, which she bothers
formally to lay . . . with starched laced linen.
And serves herself in solitary wilderness.
A lasting, unconditional and committed tribute
To love . . . to him.

The Bright Side

It must be here somewhere,
I saw it recently
Just now, just there, just everywhere . . .
But it's no good . . . not there.

And I have hunted stupidly,
in the oven, on the floor,
behind the clock, the microwave
and in my knicker drawer.

Perhaps it's in the garden
the summer house, or shed,
'anging on the clothes line,
or sitting by the bed.

Perhaps if I stop looking
it'll turn up unawares
and first thing in the morning
it'll be there on the stairs.

I really mean to find it
even though it's gone to hide
and when I look upon it . . .
I'll see The Brighter Side.

Remembering Janet.

9th April 2005

The Cost of Love

Deep in her dream she knew that voice
Unchanged through all the years . . .
Normal at first and quietly,
Somehow turned time directly into now . . .
Wake up.

So there she was, left holding this Baby of Time
noisy and obstreperous, beating the air
with clenching fists, demanding to be heard.
While the voice, drowning in misery, gone.
Come back.

Sleeping and tossing she remembered,
All the pain and all the tears,
Knowing now they were not all hers
The thundering of grieving and the demons.
The legacy of loving.

Spinning spinning she went, away in a whirlpool of empty
as winding up from the depths came two figures, long and twisting
in gym tunics of unending length, frayed girdles and school ties
catching and tearing on circling grey slime.
Bells ringing.
Pointing they were,
long accusing fingers upturned in triumph,
and turning, screeched knowing at her writhing discomfort
and wafting upwards, they were gone . . .
Into the light.

She alone, frozen in supplication
the grey walls slowly crushing her,
hideous nightmare of Godless desolation . . .
Can this truly, possibly, be the cost of love?
Please no.

Ah . . . now the Red Queen clip-clopping, hooped skirt swinging
thrusts high on the air a myriad shining lights
weaving and soaring above and around,
spilling orbs of dazzling joy . . . to settle around her.
A lapful of moments, carved in time
All is changed . . . all is the same . . . All is well.

And only now, tweaking and intrusive,
strutting Pucklike in pointy golden pumps,
trailing nonchalant a curling ribbon of doubt
winks knowing, chuckling at her lined and silver fear.
Phantom love made real.

Transfiguration

In the House dwelt a mouse
Not a mouse - but a man
Not a man - but a friend
Not a friend - but a lover.

In the lover was the glory
The glory was the House
and the House was the glory.

In the glory was the sun
In the Shining were the tears.
The tears were the mouse
that crept into the house
And the glory turned into a Star.

On the star rode a Herald
The Herald held a banner
The banner bore an image
The image was the lover -
Not the lover - but the friend
Not the friend - but the man
Not the man - but a memory
Not a memory - but a dream -

And the dream
and the star
are one.

Part IIII

The Nightmare Sequence

This is the Darkest Place

If you don't wanna go there

LOOK AWAY NOW

Black Hole

Deep in the valley, in the acrid taste of strife,
dogs grieved and whimpered and crawled away to hide,
plant-life, startled, quickly atrophied
and humans, brain dead, simply stupefied.
And there in the hole in the fetid gloom
the festering contents writhed
an hómogenous mass, breathing in the doom:
the spirit, of course, slowly died.
And the nothingness oozed a bile-laden remark
'All cats' it spewed, 'are grey in the dark.'

The Darkest Place

I don't really want to say much about my second marriage, which mercifully for all concerned, ended, without decorum, at the beginning of the nineties, after a very long, very protracted, legal battle.

What it cost in material terms was vast, everything of any value was sold to finance it; on the other hand it could be said that I was fortunate in having 'stuff' to sell.

What it all cost in physical, emotional and spiritual terms however, is immeasurable. As Petitioner I fought and paid and clawed my way out of an entirely unbelievable situation.

After his own broken marriage, my husband had come out of the Church and gone into Teaching . . . where, sickeningly, he turned his attention to his young students. I knew nothing of this of course, until he upset a mutual friend by telling him that he 'liked young girls.'

And the balloon went up . . . as it surely always does.

I, of course, turned to the Church for support. I was met by a pretty substantial brick wall. The Church closed ranks.

There was one Rural Dean who was kind to me and listened. He patiently mopped up the tears which flooded his study floor. And after several meetings he said quietly, 'It's Divorce Jane isn't it. It has to be.'

Oh, those words again. Anyway, the horribleness of the divorce came and went and of course left me shattered.

However, 'one door closes and another opens' and that is exactly what happened to me. Driving one Sunday morning up to London and half listening to Sue Lawley presenting Desert Island Discs, I was a bit interested to hear that her guest was Dr. George Carey, the Archbishop of Canterbury. And as I listened a whole new world of positivity opened up to me and the tranquil influence projected by a genuinely loving and caring human being touched my soul and gradually lifted my battered spirit. I listened carefully to everything he said but the only record I can now remember is that his favourite hymn is 'Praise to the Holiest in the Heights.' I sang along, of course. I knew every word. And with every mile covered it all became - what - more manageable I suppose. I had someone on side. I arrived in London a different, and perhaps a recovering, person.   Then I did what I always do . . . I started to write. I wrote the Archbishop a letter. I wrote carefully and truthfully - putting him in the picture and I suppose covertly asking for his help. I also wrote a long poem and, putting the whole lot into a Christmas card, addressed it to Dr and Mrs Carey and sent it off to Lambeth Palace. I'm not sure I thought it would reach the Archbishop, but it did and in the fullness of time I received a generously kind reply.

That was the time of my rebirth as a person. I have his letter still of course and look at it from time to time and it always gives me such a lift.

The poem I sent is called . . .

The Priest and the Sparrows . . . A gentle rebuke

A Fantasy for children of all ages

Sparrows are all around you
Falling . . . falling
catching in their frantic fluttering dive
moment on your hooded brambled eyes.
Bang!! Bang!! You're dead.

Look past the jerking coloured flags,
the waving, dimpled chubby hands
Look to the gaunt, stressed, tight stretched bones
calling scared, through blinking sparrow eyes
metamorph'ing as you quickly turn away.

Step back from the pleading and the battered
urging and shoving to peck at your feathered hem.
Tug at your Albert as you run up the stairs
Put it all behind you, for nobody cares -
The banqueting has begun.

What is it stopping your Hunter
as you pull on the golden chain?
Tweak - and the watch pocket vomits up
a soft brown sparrow, dead, quite dead,
caught fast in the hinge of time.

In a moment of freedom fairly rare
the boy in us all is no different in you -
you scuff through the golden leaves carpeted there
goose-stepping your wellingtons high in the air
kicking up oak leaves and crackling twigs

acorns and hazel husks - heavier bits . . .
My conker is bigger than yours.

But there in the loam of the forest floor
a small brown movement catches your eye
and the faintest mewling of faintest sound
compels you to look - against your will -
A sparrow of course, they are everywhere,
now that you're looking, on every hill . . .
And that small brown mound
in the mushroom ring
in the golden light
of the setting sun
is the place where a whole Sparrow family
Died.

'Please God, not more . . . Let this cup pass away'
you cry, in your fleecy lined gloves
as you tiptoe home
in the gathering gloom,
Squelch. There's another one gone.

In your study it's light
and the fire's burning bright
as you tear off your scarf and your togs -
you well know the answer lying deep in your soul
to this nightmare that's plaguing you
spoiling your role
You must pray, hard and fervently,
Now.

Covertly passing your flattened hand
over your hassock that's torn
it is as I said
The sound that you dread
Plop. There's another one gone.

I tell you as surely as birds are birds
don't genuflect this time, my dear,
or under your knee
like a very squashed pea
is the pulp you have now learned to fear.

'It is cold, Lord' you say, 'I am scared and alone'
'It is dark, Lord' you say, 'and I'm done,
Help me Lord, you have shown me
You really have known me
but your punishment isn't much fun.'

I will try some humility, Lord, I will,
I'll listen and hear what they say . . .
it makes my blood curdle
when I know a dead bird'll
be there every step of the way.

'I see it all now, quite plainly you see
I am here Lord to answer the call.
It's a serious matter
it wasn't just patter
when you said not one sparrow must fall.'

You are breathing more quietly now, my dear
as I leave you to think on alone
and you see in your shock
how you've treated your flock
Just be thankful the sparrows have flown.

In Streatham Woods - 1995

* * *

Days passed and the great Archbishop splendid in his robes of State slowly and with much dignity took his place in the procession.

The huge organ thundered out the opening chords, and all the people began to sing. 'Praise to the Holiest in the height' they sang, and the Archbishop listened and this time he heard, and he was very pleased.

As he walked slowly on he looked from side to side.

And this time he saw them. He saw their shining eyes and their happy faces. He saw the pain in the old man's lines and he saw the peace in the girl. And he was very pleased. He took his place at the High Altar and the big church became very still. And he felt the stillness.

The people were expectant and very quiet. The Archbishop listened and he heard the sound of their silence. And somehow, in another dimension, he understood what the people were feeling and telling him.

He listened and he heard and he was humbled and very pleased.

The great church was still . . . and still . . . and all the people bowed their heads.

Thankfully and prayerfully he held high the Host. And then . . .

High above his head - high in the rafters - he heard a fluttering. He stood tall and firm, trying not to feel the fear that crept into his heart. And all in a moment of time a small brown bird dropped onto his upstretched hands. But this time it was different.

The bird was alive. It had a pulse. The pulse of Hope. He watched.

The little bird was changing. It flew on to the very top of the heavy silver cross which stood between the candelabra on the High Altar. The Archbishop looked again at the bird and saw that it had changed into a beautiful white dove. And in a flash it was gone. But the Archbishop knew that God had listened to his prayer and had sent his answer.

The Archbishop was happy and he knew that he had learned a very big lesson from the small brown bird.

He had learned that he must listen.

Likewise after supper he took the cup . . .

Lambeth Palace London SE1 7JU

4 January 1996

Dear Jane,

Thank you so much for your kind letter, together with the wonderful poem you sent. I am very sorry of course for the break-up of your marriage but I am glad that Andrew Nunn, one of my staff has been handling some of your questions sensitively. We all have to live with the Church as it is - imperfect, stumbling and often graceless; but we all need it - including Archbishops!

I do want to encourage you in your pilgrimage and especially not to give up hoping, praying, believing and trusting. Your poem shows you have a great skill in crafting words and perhaps this is something you should develop in the days to come. Let me urge you to continue with your writing! Thank you for it and I trust that this Archbishop at least is listening!

With good wishes and prayers for 1996.

Yours sincerely,

+ George Cantuar

The Spin Off

And that was that . . . or should have been. The marriage was dissolved and the Decree stated that . . . 'The Respondent has behaved in such a way, that the Petitioner cannot reasonably be expected to live with the Respondent.' And it doesn't get much clearer than that. Job done. Finito.

However, there is, of course, always a dwindling, curling stream of events. And so there was in this case. Two things emerged to grapple with. First - and rather strangely, there was guilt and oddly, my guilt. For a long time I lived with this on a daily basis. I had not actually exposed him outside of the Court. The Court knew all the facts, of course. It was upon the facts that their findings were based. Surely, they would have taken it further had it been deemed necessary? But he was still 'out there', and I had kids. Should I have told someone - the Headmaster - and let him decide? The Police and let them? And I had not.

I was completely exhausted after years of fighting the case and there was much to do. I know he has had one further failed marriage and one relationship, so he has been fairly busy since my incumbency and he is pretty old now, so we may hope he has learned something. Oh dear. How screwed up can you get?

I find I cannot go to church any more and I do miss the corporate worship. Perhaps that is my penance. My punishment. 'Divorce is always a tragedy - no one wins - everybody loses.'

Secondly, beloved friends and their possible loss. This is a devastating issue. Dear long term friends who find themselves in the unenviable position of having divided loyalties. Only one way to deal with this. That is to come clean . . . to spill the beans.

Not easy. Not British. Forcing them to face up too, which is so not what they want to be doing.

My poems 'Windmill' and 'Ficus' endeavour to address and reflect this aspect of the Spin Off.

And now, really, that is quite enough of all of that.

Windmill

That chap who wrote, 'Behold a giant am I,
aloft here in my tower' . . .
was not really talking about bread, you know.
No, like Alice, he thought he might be perceived
as addressing the Primary intake . . .
that host of apple cheeked Just Williams,
who, in their captive role
confront, in their temporary misery,
the tedium of poetry by rote.
But I saw through him long ago. Oh yes.

Hiding in his appointed imagery
he told us of himself - upon whatever level.
'It's up to you,' he said, 'how you see me.
I'm a fair big heavy built chap
I planted mesel' 'ere, must be sixty year on
now,
an' I jest stays put.
It's nae bad on this hill
I tek what comes along -
wen wind blows I cetch a thing or two,
some I swallow - some I throw back on th'air
And when I've had enough I switches off.

But that is not you, I thought at first it was.
I see you more as .... a lighthouse.
You and me both.
Two lighthouses, planted in granite,
observing each the other
like David and Goliath . . . from two opposing rocks
across a turgid sea of divided loyalties.
'I'm guiding in the other ship', you boomed
That hurt. And I minded.
But when all, all is hurting
a toothache, more or less, just does not signify.

So here we stand
Far off enough for total isolation
Near in enough for total desolation
Confusion swirling high round our rocky footholds,
That neither dog nor fish can get aboard

to pee upon our slippery, shiny roots.
Ships pass.

Consider your form.
No sails. No granite jaws.
You cannot wave.
A galleried eyebrow only Jonathan can land upon . . .
He, busy with his solitary quest,
pecks at the glass and softly glides away
. . . The glass? What glass? . . .
'Oh God . . . the light.
You . . . have . . . a . . . light.'

Think about light.
Progression into light.
Light of Light.
Light of Love.
Light of Friendship.
And a Light to lighten the Gentiles.
Light and Dark.
Harbour Lights.
Lighten our Darkness.
Headlights.
Footlights.
Stage lights.
Lights on. Lights off.
Flashing lights.
Strobe lights.
Rotating lights.
Signal lights.
That's it. Rotating signal lights.

Back! Back! Back!
Back to your memberless form
Deep inside - beneath your galleried eyebrow
Your motor ticks away the hours
Frozen in an unbidden warp of time.
I need to know about your motor.
I care. I really care.
Send me a beam of light.

Like you I cannot speak.
Like you I cannot wave.
Like you I cannot move.
More words, like you, I neither want nor need.
But before the ice-white, gull dropped stalactites
cover and distort your light . . .
Send me a beam.

Once, then, I was your friend
and because you were, you are.
Do this one thing for me
your one time friend . . .
or I shall simply, slowly . . . bow my head.

7th February 1993   For Brian

Ficus

And then, as if all that were not enough -
All that uneasy silence
All that pain
All that, that lay between us
like a sort of spongy blob . . .
the kind of thing upon a shore
kids gingerly prod at with their toes
or build into their sand fort
or set upon a totem and dance around . . .
Not knowing like Pandora knew,
the intricacies that in it dwelt,
and grew.

So then, if that were not enough, for Heaven's sake,
the Ficus began to die.
No reason why.
You remember the Ficus, you must . . .
chosen with such care
planted with such love,
and borne here on a rare and golden day;
and placed with ceremony, without a sign of strife,
It grew and flourished and loved life.

And like the ten foot salmon
or the fourteenth hole in one
became a kind of symbol of all that we had done.
Always admired, always discussed,
always there . . . the voiceless bond.
And like the kids upon the shingle
though more languid in approach
the grownups laughed and in their turn
poked at the compost there,
drew glistening foliage through caring fingers . . .
and went away well pleased . . .
'It's doing well,' the grownups said,
'It likes this home, this air . . .
The light is right, look at the height . . .
It's all very good,' they purred.
And still the Ficus - preening - grew.
And knew.

Then came the wind of change,
and darkness over all the earth
darker than the darkest night
and rolling ever on . . .
huge bruise - black clouds inked in the sun -
eclipsed, the light was gone.

Sparrows in their fright took flight
and in the unaccustomed night
collided with their neighbours' friends
in frenzied plea to make amends
fell powerless, wingless to their ends.
And as upon the count of ten
the hordes withdrew . . . they knew.
They had seen it all before . . .
This war.

Now the all seeing, cosseted Ficus,
Observing all that from its pill box slit
Dodging the mortar thrown missiles
avoiding the doodlebug shit . . .
reared in love and weaned on chat
couldn't be doing with all of that . . .
drew over itself for its own good
a very original kind of hood,
a big Barracuda sort of thing
and safe therein, like a kind of hat . . .
It sat.

But as any half a gardener knows
it encouraged the Ficus to turn up its toes.
And predictably, as here implied
The Ficus Variegata died.

For Anne

For Brian - after his op

I'm rejoicing, now Ann's told me
I am singing (would I could)
I am just so bloody thankful
with the news, so bloody good.

Now just listen, new young Brian,
Listen now and listen good,
Though you may not want to hear it
I who'm older think you should.

All the time you were disabled
I, quite rightly, played it cool,
When a friend of mine is poorly,
Peace and rest's the golden rule.
Now you're out intensication
Now you give no cause for alarm,
 I reveal my perspication
now I know it won't do harm.

I'm a Leo sitting purring,
waiting for just such a pause
you should know, as if you didn't,
Big cats always sharpen claws.
Lions, wondrous, glorious creatures
waiting, wash behind their ears
give impression false security,
mice and men allay their fears.

But you should be ever watchful
Lionesses bide their time
and, you golden blue-eyed cherub,
recognise this day is mine.
Remember? I'm the old appendage
You so cruelly set aside
feeling in some puerile cop-out
I was on an easy ride.

So now flexing, tendons gleaming,
outraged, set the record straight
even if your last reaction
is a fireball of hate.
First off, let me make the point, it's
not your body bronze I seek,
No my dear, I tell you frankly,
I'd prefer a nice Antique.

No, it's just through all the trauma
Need to tell you how I feel
Angry that you thought I came as
just part of a Package Deal.
I'm a person, standing proudly,
if you bothered, you would find
underneath the outer wrapping
though concealed, there is a mind.

Don't you think I understand it
understand too bloody well
That through all the years that follow
I shall miss you both like hell?

Now I've made the point and said it
Having done, I feel quite sad . . .
Realise our tenuous friendship
could now go from fair to bad.

All I know is, now and ever
Everybody's mind is free
So, in case all links we sever,
Please just think of me as ME.

Windmill, Ficus and After the Op.

Brian and Anne were our best friends. Windmill expresses the awfulness of divided loyalties. Brian wrote a charming response setting out the difficulties for all concerned. He got it.

Ficus I read to Anne one day as it contained the reality of the situation - and she had given me the plant. And of course After the Op was a joke. I suppose I was saying, 'I'm still here.' 'Help me.' 'Love me.'

It was a bad time. Hard for all of us.

It resolved, of course, as things invariably do. The protagonist took to the hills never to be seen again. And gently and surely things got back to normal - whatever that is. Our friendship continued on a three legged basis.

Thank you God.

And sadly - more than sadly - we lost Brian soon afterwards.

Too soon.

Too young.

Brian Merrick 25th September 2006

Brian and Anne

Today in watery Autumn sun
I picked two roses white . . .
one taller than the other . . .
and joined at hip of stem,
one for you and one for him.

Then in my solitude,
I sat and watched and listened
and I perceived it all,
just as I knew it would be . . .
A salutation to a great man.

And listening through my tears
his voice showed me a focus . . .
not on today, this happening
but only on the good . . .
good thoughts, good times, great wisdom.

And I smiled a watery smile.

74

Shopping for a Car – A Hymn to Brian

On an evening late in winter
When the fog lay thick and swirling
Swirled it thickly o'er the river
and the trees which lay beside it,
shrouded they in ghostly silence
densely dripping in the darkness.
And the river moving sluggish
soundless sucking at the seabirds,
whispers wordless in its motion.

Moving lightly through the darkness,
Snapping leaf wood as he passes
comes a figure light and shining
and about him is a glowing
head held high and tresses flowing -
eyes ashine and features smiling -
Here the noble Thane of Lympstone
(though his roots lie deep in Eire)
comes in striding from the forest.
And his leather, strapped about him
holding fast his long days booty.

But his bosom holds a secret
joyful secret, no one knowing -
folding to him such a wonder
quiet knowledge of his jewel,
came he in, his whole form glowing.

In the firelight sat his maiden
smiling shyly from the shadow -
passes him a steaming kop she
turns to give him of the sheepskin.
'I have found this day a treasure
such a sight as never man saw
came upon her on the sudden
far upon the heights of Kastner.
By her side sit many dragons
spitting flames and shifting boulders -
Siren singing on the hillside
And her name is Mitsu Bishi.

75

Then his maiden in a flurry
begs, beseeches - arms akimbo -
'Do not scale the heights of Kastner
Do not look upon the glitter -
Who will bring the wood for fire 'n
Who will feed the braves in winter
Who will keep the wolves from portal?
Do not look upon the jewel
Leave the flaming Mitsu Bishi'.

Then the noble Thane of Lympstone
reels bewildered by the thought,
wrings his hands and beats his chest, he
wonders at the hell he's wrought -
Face looks gloomy, forehead frowning
Head is bowed and cheek is pale -
Can it be he has mistaken
Mitsu for the Holy Grail?

Soft with love the words come calmly
now she sees her lord in pain
'We have only moved our campsite,
we have only fed the braves.
Need we of the golden switch - bitch,
need we of her power and woe?
We can always hire a Watha
if our grey Ford will not go'.

More in sorrow than in anger
steps once more into the cold
deep within his soul still linger
visions of his crock of gold.
Burst to action on the flower drums
lying idle in the mire -
Summons now his worthy Chieftains,
him with truth they will inspire.

Far away they hear his calling -
drumming through the rain and mist -
drop the arrowheads they're carving
jump to heed the call, though pissed.
Stepping forward from the forest
in a poppy seeded haze

smiles his friend, Titus a Toe Rag
ere his eyes begin to glaze.

Follows close upon his heels, he
flicks his fingers and behold
staggers to the fore his soul-mate,
Hot Lips Rosie with a cold.

This could be a maxi Ho - Ho,
Titus gently taps his nose
Leads the others to make pow - wow
genuflecting as he goes.
Seated round the local camp fire
flagons filled and feathers fine,
Titus makes astute suggestions,
Rosie sinks to a decline.

Through the many hours of daylight
daylight changed to dark en route,
round the circle all the comment
Pipe of Peace in hot pursuit.
All the 'yes buts' and the 'well ands'
'in the light ofs' sagely put
this strange foursome ventures, dropping,
Go to have another look.

Here the Thane takes up the cudgel
His the fight to slay the foe
Gently adjures that his maiden
Step not in where he should go.

Soon he gains the Heights of Kastner -
Looking up - he sees no star,
But he knows that Mitsubishi
Ain't no ordinary car.

Sheila and Lee

You told me. . .
'When I leave him,
Bend to kiss his cheek
He looks at me.'

Why you think,
'He blames me?'
I think you know,
Events not you.

When you hear him say,
'Why am I here?'
I think deep down, you know . . .
He knows.

Why DO you think he's saying
'It's your fault?'
I think it not the case,
Relief is more.

Of course he looks at you,
Through eyes now dimmed by time,
He wants to see you.

Of course he does not blame,
He looks and blame is his.
His worry is for you.

And when you touch his cheek . . .
The touch is sweet.
He knows you love him.

And when you hold his hand,
He feels concern for you,
Of love enfolding both.

Listen to your heart,
not wait for words unspoke;
but trust in all you know.

Accept this bitter pill
and though the taste be raw,
step through into the gift of Now.
Become again the girl he knew.

Min dear, Brandy and? Whisky and? Gin and?

Book Launch

The Book . . . Hannah's Ghost . . . Author Ann Merrick

Even the sea has gone,
that one last dependable utterness
Gone.
The cliffs and Golden Cap -
A figment - gone.

There is only a backdrop
a soggy greyness, held by a Deity
too bored or too tired even to hold it straight
looped and sagging - merging
with the no sky.
And not the slightest lapping.
Forward or back . . ?
A black nose edges into my glove
and a small fluff scrabbles at my knees.
'Come back,' they say.

None of this is their fault.
Nor is it of their making
'I will feed them first' I thought
and then we'll see.

Turning back, away from the impenetrable shroud -
rain swirling at my hair and teasing as I wept
the cloud mass parted . . . and there
a patch of piercing yellow
momentary, but enough.

'It will be all right. It will,' I thought -
and tomorrow is another day.
And so it is. Snowy and warm.
And I can see the hills and sense the yellow.

This is your day. Your book is launched -
and I so proud and pleased.
'If Hannah can grapple with her ghost,' I thought,
'Then let me set about mine.'

1982 - Darkness

Oh no please, not war again. The News, The Today Programme . . . all full of it. And it all started so quietly. A few Argentineans had landed on the Falkland Islands. For what reason? And with evil intent? The Falklands, where exactly are they? But I don't like the drums of war - so I listened intently. Oh right . . . the other side of the world . . . But they're British with British citizens. Jump to it. And Argentina is just next door across . . .

And then my mother was on the phone, 'how wonderful is Margaret Thatcher an' all, rallying the troops and setting sail to the other side of the world...'

The World Service took up the story, so now I was listening day AND night. I'm sure I don't know what it was all actually about . . . but there had to be an Agenda. Money . . . Oil . . . World Domination? The Falklands had to be defended at all costs and so did the Britons who dwelt there.

But in 100 years, no one living there now would be alive. Why not tell the Brits that in a hundred years the Falklands would be handed over, or back, to Argentina and to make plans accordingly? Of course, that's all far too simplistic.

But at the same time many Brits had Argentinean wives or husbands and families . . . after all they were neighbours and that's what happens. Was it really worth a war? Well, yes, obviously it was. It couldn't just have been the people . . . could it? In any event it was clearly vastly important to defend and hold that territory - which was done - swiftly and decisively. A few months . . . five, six? And it was all over.

A Clean War.

But by the time it was all over and our servicemen returning victorious, I had other more pressing domestic worries . . .

My mother became ill.

I visited her quite normally one afternoon and found she had taken to sleeping downstairs. A most unlikely move for her to have made. Why would she do that? I rang her doctor and asked him to call . . . and before anyone knew it she was in the Cottage Hospital at Butleigh. By a stroke of very good fortune my sister was down from Scotland and sadly and totally unbelievably, we were very soon arranging our mother's funeral in the village church. It all happened so quickly . . . swiftly and decisively.

A few days . . . five, six? And it was all over.

A Kind Death.

'A wonderful way to go' they said.

But what does that mean for Heaven's sake. I can't agree. I was there and I don't think so. And mothers are immortal. They don't just hop off without so much as a 'by ya leave.' Even if they are 81.

She was a constant large presence. Thoughtful, humorous, controversial and a force to be reckoned with and I couldn't stand it.

I wanted her there.

I wanted her on the phone.

I wanted her light.

Olive Lily Bennett. 1901 - 1982.

Olive

A little light went out the other day,
Like a leaf, let go, that fluttered down,
Like teeth that drop in near dead dark . . .
It's quiet now, that light, that leaf,
that little life.

Not much of a light, quite small,
not much of a life . . .
'Thank you,' it said, and died.
Thank you - I ask you - thank you -
Thank you to whom, to what?
Thank you drug?
Thank you Nurse?
Thank you Lord?
A small unheeded word
only I heard it . . .Thank you
Thank you it said . . . and died.

But it was not always thus.
Time was it sang - it really sang
with nothing much to sing about, it sang
so that ladies passing with their babies
and their baskets, stopped to listen.
The man who bore the milk, two churns upon a yoke
stopped in his ponderous tracks, wondering at the sound
Some there must be who heard it,
dusting and doing she sang -
How she could sing!
How could she sing - My God - for what?
In war-wracked garden, with dog fights overhead -
'Wait you men fools, hold, my baby's there'
picked gently up the shawl folds - fat pink cheeks,
then, 'Right, on now, but if you must,
fight quietly, this doesn't need to hear'
and singing, lulled that little back to sleep.

Time was - those old legs ran,
not only ran, but raced her children barefoot
over daisies low to cut -
soft mossy grass between her short young toes
Time was we all played cricket
with red hot poker stems for stumps
but worriedly, 'The lupin bed's behind you,
We'll go on with this another day . . . I've won.
Time was . . . time was . . . it's gone.

Yesterday came suddenly . . .

Yesterday, all my troubles seemed so far away,

Now it looks as though they're here to stay,

Oh, I believe in yesterday.

Suddenly, I'm not half the man I used to be,

There's a shadow hanging over me,

Oh yesterday came suddenly . . .

Why she had to go, I don't know. She wouldn't say.

I said something wrong, now I long for yesterday.

Yesterday, love was such an easy game to play,

Now I need a place to hide away,

Oh, I believe in yesterday . . .

Lennon & McCartney 1965

85

Part V

But don't be too sad . . .

For just around the corner . . .

Are Lilies . . . Beautiful Lilies

Enter

Lily . . . The Belle Lily

10 Years on - Lily Brooks 13.04.1992

Ten Years On

Olive Lily Bennett 20th January 1901 - 1982

Lily Brooks 13th April 1992 -

I sat once in a darkened room
watching while you slept.
And as you slept,
I fretted
and worried
and somehow smiled.
The smile to keep you unafraid . . .
The smile I did not feel.

Yet in that wavering sleep
I saw you quite composed.
I feared that you would go
I worried you would know –
But it was for me I minded.

And as the light faded
so ebbed that little life . . .
still so much left unsaid
still gardening to do
still furniture to move.
Calm in a small white unaccustomed bed.

Time passed
and unshed tears
turned to unseen stone.
Cared still that you had gone
leaving me unprepared.
A heavy space left empty.

But now I see it all . . .
As quiet I watch in wonder here,
like a peony unfolding near,
New life . . .
flails at the air with fast clenched fists
battles with head, too heavy yet to lift . . .

New life that meant to be

. . . But the eyes, the timeless eyes
deep mirrors of all seeing blue
stare back unblinking
and I knew
old Olive, true, has stepped aside
but in Lily she is with us still.
The Loving Spirit meant to be . . .
And unquenched dances on.

Jane

In the Rookery Gardens

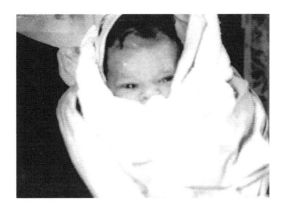

Packed Lunch   18th December 1995   Lily was 3 ½

On Tuesday morning Lily was busy
She was preparing her Lunch Box.
Packed Lunch is fun, grown up and important.

And so I thought, in packed lunch terms . . .
Lily is a jaffa cake
soft round and tasty, with a surprising core.
A closed circuit, ready to roll.
Everyone loves a Jaffa Cake.

Amanda is a slim brown finger sandwich
of smoked salmon.
Luscious, sensuous, elegant and rare.
You must appreciate smoked salmon . . .
It's an acquired taste. Take care.

Ma is a Lion Bar. Forbidden fruit
Big - take your time - there's plenty.
Saccharin sweet - coated in glamour -
but mind the jagged nuts
They bite if you hurt . . . or hurt if you bite.

There's my packed lunch.
A glorious mix.
An homogeny of fun, fantasy
and fat, a dash of fear,
A close knot . . . all part of the
whole
And tightly wrapped in
clingfilm.

Merry Christmas,
I would like to share this poem with ypu.

What is life?
What is life I do not know,
I'm searching high and low.
Up in the sky where the stars do shin
I,e is my awnser there to find,
In my space ship i'll fly up,
In the stars i'll try my luck..
For way up there we each have a star and
that star is looking down on YOU.

Lily Brooks - 9 years
(spelling mistakes and typos courtesy of Lily)

Easter Prize Virgo Fidelis School

I think about you Jesus, at this time of the year
Suffering to keep the world going round.
People go without things to try and be like you.
Forty days and forty nights . . .
we'll never be like you
Whatever we give up we still have
our families
our beds,
and a nice house to live in.
But you were all alone in the wilderness.
Thankyou, Jesus,
for giving up your life
for our world.

Lily Brooks. Age 10

These are my days

I sit alone in the coffee shop,
watching people laugh.
Mothers attending to their young ones:
Sometimes days are good, others bad.
Folk think I'm strange . . .
an old lady as rich as I am
sitting every day in the same place.

People don't know how lucky they are
having family and friends around, laughing,
sharing their worries.
But I look into the mirror,
and what do I see?
A sad old woman looking back at me.

People come and people go
I can't make friends,
I don't know how . . .
I keep myself to myself . . .
and let people get on with it.
These are my days . . .
For the rest of my life.

Lily Brooks Age 12

Love

Love surrounds us with Hope and Joy
Bringing people together.
Never fear, for you're never alone,
You've got the power of Love within.
Love will never leave your side . . .
whatever you may say . . .
wherever you may go . . .
Love overflows all streams,
Conquers hate and defeats all evil.
Never wait for love to come to you.
It will always be there.

Lily Brooks Age 11
Virgo Fidelis

Part VI

Inappropriate Marriages

Broken Hearts

Lessons Learned

If I fell . . .

If I fell in love with you
Would you promise to be true
And help me understand
'Cause I've been in love before
And I found that love was more
Than just holding hands

If I give my heart to you
I must be sure
From the very start
That you would love me more than her

If I trust in you oh please
Don't run and hide
If I love you too oh please
Don't hurt my pride like her

'Cause I couldn't stand the pain
And I would be sad if our new love was in vain

So I hope you see that I
Would love to love you
And that she will cry
When she learns we are two
If I fell in love with you

Hmmmmm ....

Sad ....

Been there ....

Done that ....

Lennon and McCartney 1964

96

What was your name?

He said:
I loved you then, I always have.
She held him.
They did not kiss - they knew the rules
And all so very long ago.
She sighed . . .

He said:
RYB1, do you remember?
The XK - long, low and powerful.
Fast cars. That and all the others
Oh, yes! She remembered.
She smiled . . .

He said:
We will find the hill, our field -
walked primrose through to clover
and dreamed long dreams of love,
in time without time - love the only reality.
She glowed . . .

He said:
Even now I have your gifts.
The twinkling eye of yesterday
And he had brought her perfume then
long ago - Je Reviens - and so he had.
She mused . . .

He said:
I know that music - They're singing our song
I'll come over - We'll have lunch
He did not come, of course
Too soon, she thought.
She waited . . .

And then he spoke no more
The endless past returned
She grappled confusion and, reluctantly, rejection.
Only a cold pervasive silence.
And in that moment innocence had died.
She wept no more.

Starting Over

God, it's scary . . .
Can the bliss that was
times two
banish the fear that is
times one . . .
or maybe two, who knows . . .

You think too much, he said,
then and now.
Move on, let it all go . . .
and maybe I do, think too much, that is
but, no, it's scary, O.K?

F'rinstance, he came the other day,
bearing gifts . . .
This gateau, voluptuous it was, of course
with a ballet skirt of cream . . .
festooned with glazed strawberries
cupped in more cream . . .
Sin in cellophane.

And I had this vision
of a single long - stemmed white rose
calorie free, symbol of tranquillity
and I knew
that if we should fall in love again
which of course couldn't happen,
well, it could . . . but unlikely,
possible, I s'pose, but improbable
fun perhaps, but far too scary . . .

But just supposing we did . . .
fall in love, I mean . . .
then I knew the single long - stemmed white rose
would simply, quietly metamorph, to red.
Oh God, but it's scary . . . believe me.

Birthdays

Quote:
'You didn't come. You didn't call. You didn't phone.'
It's my turn now to raise it,
But you won't get away with it,
This time I'll make you face it.

You've got the situation wrong,
You've jumped the wrong conclusion,
This time it's not of love, my song,
Away with this confusion.

It wasn't I summoned the past
It wasn't I approached you . . .
I would have driven off quite fast
Had I foreseen the long view.

I've seen you over all these years,
I passed without detection . . .
But now my eyes aren't filled with tears
And I avoid rejection.

I've seen you in your red striped shirt
and in the throes of dealing . . .
I've seen you moving in your cars
whilst my own face concealing.

I've seen you with your shock of hair
It isn't you I'm seeking
I haven't even stopped to stare
I've just gone on Antique-ing.

You said 'I'll keep in touch with you,
I'll ring you on a Friday' . . .
Those are the words you'll come to rue . . .
Tomorrow could be MY day.

One day I'll look into your eyes
It's not a day I'll hasten,
But sometime soon, before time flies
I'll have an explanation.

99

Ballad

What did I mean to you?
I really need to know
Rides in fast cars
Love under the stars
Is that all I was to you?

What did I mean to you?
And will I ever know?
A romp in the hay
On a summer day
Is that all I was to you?

What did I mean to you?
I will always want to know
Close on the hill
When the world was still
Is that all I was to you?

What did I mean to you?
I expect I will never know
A stolen night
Well out of sight
Is that all I was to you?

And what were you to me?
And who can I ever tell?
Kisses like wine
When you came into dine
That's what you were to me.

And what were you to me?
And how can I ever say?
A broken heart
When we were apart
That's what you were to me.

And what were you to me?
And will I forget to recall?
That closeness begun
When we were one
That's what you were to me.

And what were you to me?
And who will ever know?
The pain and the tears
Inexpressible fear
That's what you were to me.

1968 4.2 LITRE XJ6

Strangely, after all the years . . .

You said you loved me
in the greyness of our years
You said you loved me . . . and
Strangely, I find myself profoundly sad.

Of course, within my head,
Far off bells clang tinkling
as dreams and phantom memory
drag kicking, into now.

You said you loved me
in the greyness of our years
You said you loved me . . . and
Strangely, my draining fear is absolute.

Why sad . . . ?
Sad for the lifetime of living
swamped in the clay toil of being
Gone in the twinkling of a failing eye,
Time, not wasted, but lost.

And fear . . . why fear?
Fear from forgotten maiden days
and hugely component of love
truncated now, in every fussy detail . . .
afraid of fear, always the exquisite bar.

But the words are said . . .
In the greyness of our years
You said you loved me.
And therefore, we can bounce
and jump and dance and spin
and fly together into a setting haze of trust
as long as you will hold me by the hand.
Because of course, in simple terms . . . and
Strangely, after all the years, I love you still.

Right off you

I'm stopping all this faffing about
fluffy cloud thoughts in the stillness
murmuring nothings in the blackness
remembering.

My head is telling me . . . pack it in,
get on with few minutes of life
you might have left.
Get over it.

Anyway, I don't believe
I even like you now
discourteous, dismissive, unjust, cold
grown up boy.

Oh, but I did love the boy
It's the man I'm dumping.
Forty years . . . pathetic or what
It could just take a while.

Love - Just one of those things

It was just one of those things
Just one of those crazy flings
One of those bells that now and then rings
Just one of those things

It was just one of those nights
Just one of those fabulous flights
A trip to the moon on gossamer wings
Just one of those things

If we'd thought a bit, of the end of it
When we started painting the town
We'd have been aware that our love affair
Was too hot, not to cool down

So good-bye, dear, and amen
Here's hoping we meet now and then
It was great fun
But it was just one of those things
Just one of those things

Cole Porter 1935

LEAVE

ME

ALONE . . .

Off the hook - 14th August 1992

It is tranquil here and calm . . .
Such calm I had forgotten –
There is peace around
and quiet in the soul.

The air is fresh here now
it tastes of dew and Spring time . . .
You can hear the silence here
The splashing as the water boatman jumps . . .
The shattering sound of leaves dropping . . .
Noisy butterflies in the buddleia . . .
Raindrops plopping loudly . . .
Huge sounds you haven't heard for long.

We are high, high, high, we are gliding.
We are singing, singing, singing out of tune.
Like the sun we are smiling, smiling, smiling.
We are dancing, dancing, dancing,
dancing dancing on your grave!

Hey Jude

Hey Jude, don't make it bad.
Take a sad song and make it better.
Remember to let her into your heart,
Then you can start to make it better.

Hey Jude, don't be afraid.
You were made to go out and get her.
The minute you let her under your skin,
Then you begin to make it better.

And anytime you feel the pain, hey Jude, refrain,
Don't carry the world upon your shoulders.
For well you know that it's a fool who plays it cool
By making his world a little colder.

Hey Jude, don't let me down.
You have found her, now go and get her.
Remember to let her into your heart,
Then you can start to make it better.

So let it out and let it in, hey Jude, begin,
You're waiting for someone to perform with.
And don't you know that it's just you, hey Jude, you'll do,
The movement you need is on your shoulder.

Hey Jude, don't make it bad.
Take a sad song and make it better.
Remember to let her under your skin,
Then you'll begin to make it better better better better, oh.

Lennon & McCartney 1968

First Love

So now is widowing time
and all those years from
trysting until death
assume a quiet air.

Unbidden tears surprise me
and kindly memory
rejects abundant turmoil
in sorrow for your fear.

Stanley William Brooks
R.I.P 20th September 2000

2001 - A Stark Lunacy

I can smell the burning
black acrid in my senses . . .
Brace up, you'd say,
Think of other things
Listen to the World Service
droning on . . .
It isn't the burning.

Cooking, you'd say.
It can't be the cooking . . .
Frozen dinner for one
leave in the bag
microwave 12 minutes.
It isn't the cooking.

Linen, you'd say.
It can't be the linen.
Smooth clean sheets folded away
man made fibre, 40 per cent
dried upstairs on a sagging line
cannot absorb . . .
It isn't the linen.

Too far, you'd say.
Think of other things.
Listen to the World Service
droning on telling of sacrificial pyres.

I can smell the burning.
And I am sobbing.

'2001 . . . A STARK LUNACY' . . . was generated by a foot and mouth outbreak, which hit the U.K, in 2001. Amazingly, Dorset was unaffected, but I was in Scotland at the time and there I witnessed the full horror of the impact of the disease. I had heard of the multiple burning of thousands of sheep and cattle, but it had to be seen to be believed.

Scotland is a wild and beautiful country with vast stretches of open moorland as far as the eye can see. Through this wilderness meanders the little road. Normally the gasps are gasps of delight, when taking in the vistas of beauty surrounding the traveller. However, when I was there that year, those gasps were of dismay and I have to say, of horror. It was true then, all that unbelievable news that was coming out daily on the radio.

There, across the fields and hedgerows, beyond the meadows swaying with a maze of flora in colour, just far off enough for decency, were the fires . . . The pyres consuming abandoned bodies, thrown and bundled every whichway, to feed the flames. I didn't like that.

Rachel and I were on our annual pilgrimage to visit the brother . . . normally such a happy occasion, but this time it was different. This time there was all this carnage. We went into shock.

We had been brought up in the quiet of the New Forest - too quiet sometimes of course, for a couple of kids wanting to spread their wings - but environment rubs off. Here we had learned to care for and nurture our animals and to respect them, even the Forest Ponies had their place. And they had, and have, Rights.

In those days before the War, the Forest was not fenced. Traffic on the A3I which ran through Hampshire was still fairly sparse, and the ponies and sometimes donkeys rambled freely. I believe there were some tragic accidents in which the vehicles invariably came off worse . . . but the Ponies had Rights. They had the Right of the Road.

Even after all these years, I can still almost hear my father's voice booming in the darkness. 'Come on all of you. Coats on, boots on. Down here. Now. Move. Prepare to repel boarders. Usual drill. Spread out. Go.' We knew the drill all right. We had a garden full of ponies, all over the roses and consuming the vegetables where the father had been 'Digging for Victory.'

It was always freezing cold (they seldom came in the summer, there was food enough outside,) and dragged from our warm beds we spread out and in a pincer movement, quickly cleared the brutes. We did not always love them.

And so, years later, in Scotland, faced with the horror of Foot and Mouth, we reacted like Country Girls. Speaking later to a scientist, I understood that the animals actually recover from the disease, as humans do from 'Flu, but that they cannot then go into the food chain. So it was all about money then, like so much else. I didn't verify this information, so it may or may not be true. But it was good enough for me. I had smelt the burning.

Salutation to the Dawn

Believed to be a translation from the original Sanskrit

Listen to the exhortation of the Dawn . . .

Look to this day - for it is Life

The very Life of Life.

In its brief course lie all the verities

And realities of your existence . . .

The Glory of Action . . .

The Bliss of Growth . . .

The Splendour of Beauty . . .

For yesterday is but a dream,

And tomorrow is only a vision.

But today well lived, makes

Every yesterday a dream of Happiness

And every tomorrow a vision of Hope.

Look well therefore, to this Day.

Such is the Salutation to the Dawn.

Taken on Rachel's 21st Birthday, 1961

Rachel

If you came this way, taking the road that you would have taken (that was going to be something like the beginning of Little Gidding, but I never could get it right) so I shall go on without it.

However, if you came this way with me, along the A35 for a couple of miles and then turn left into the lanes and up onto the hills, the Hardy hills, you would see where Tess walked. I have seen her up there often . . . well not often, twice.

Walking with Tess is a strange experience, but special and privileged. She is always in a fluster, but going along on the rough ground determined to get there, and in those boots. It is such a long way to Stonehenge . . .

This is a special part of Dorset, quiet and beautiful. And the Gorse is always in bloom. Always one little bush, somewhere up there. You know about 'I will love you as long as the Gorse is in bloom', don't you? Be careful what you wish for . . . that's a lifelong commitment.

Anyway, going all along the ridge, up and down the hills, round the bends in the lanes which follow the hedges and boundaries of the fields, when horses were the only mode of transport . . . or you walk . . . like Tess.

Passing through a couple of lazy villages, beside verges crowded with primroses in their time and followed by massed waving bluebells in theirs, you will finally come to Cerne Abbas (of Giant fame? but we won't go there). And Rachel, for that is where she lived.

Cerne Abbas is ancient, with a mixture of lovely houses and cottages, all of different periods and it sports a Post Office and a shop or two, some selling paintings, of course, and trinkets and crafts of local interest. There are tearooms too, to cope with the influx of tourists who drizzle along at all times of the year.

Rachel is my little sister, all growed up. She was the Blitz baby you may remember, the one who followed . . . later. We were fortunate in living fairly close . . . 20 miles or so, and we saw each other most weeks.

We had always got on like a house on fire, well you would wouldn't you, when you had gone through a war together, although she was born a year after it started. She just remembered being frightened when the noise of a bomb whistled down the chimney. I was frightened too, as I grabbed her.

On this particular day something was not quite right, different, unusual. Rachel had followed in the family footsteps of contracting Arthritis at a fairly early age . . . but hers was of the far more aggressive variety, Rheumatoid Arthritis, and she was in fairly constant and progressive pain.

But it wasn't that on this particular day. It was something more and of course I noticed at once. 'What's up darling?' I said, after lunch. 'What matter you?' And it all came out. Quite quietly she told me she had been finding it difficult to co-ordinate and had been diagnosed with Parkinson's disease. She was under 60. She soldiered on as long as possible with loving family and carers to help her . . . but inevitably, finally, she needed round the clock care and went into a nursing home.

It was a completely devastating time, for her, for all of us.

'I really don't want to end up dribbling in a corner,' she said, 'not knowing anyone, or my own name.' It was a terrible truth she was facing, so bravely and so quietly, as was her way.

At least she was spared that indignity. She died two years later. She was 66. But I have planted primroses on her grave.

She always loved them so.

A Trilogy for

Rachel

20.09.40 - 08.04.07

... fly free

A Sibling Hurting

What matter you, where you gone?
Don't go, please don't go.
What happen you, and when and why?
Don't let it happen... please don't go.

You alarm me, looking out from your shell,
do you know the sea sounds worse
when you listen through a shell . . .
Stamp on the shell.

When did the cobwebs close around you,
darkening your vision,
tying your hands,
closing your ears?
Cobwebs grow but are combustible . . .
So here's a match.

I know your body hurts like hell
but the mind and the spirit
are stronger than the hurting bones.
Can you catch the moment?
Give Hope a chance.

Before the pain the will was weakening
remember when you had the will... the strength?
You know what happens when you overwind a spring
or blow too long into a round balloon . . .
It bursts, don't burst.

Could you stamp a lot, or cry
or even break a plate or seven
or tell me loudly when I'm talking tripe
and why don't I shut up?

Or could you talk to me
and tell me where it hurts . . .
Could you vomit up the pain and grapple,
you know I'll help.

Sweet sibling, you are so much loved,
you are my small Blitz baby grown.
I laughed at your first stumbling steps
take them again for me.

I'm here for you, like then
outstretched arms extended,
I will not let you fall, I dare not let you fall
I have the Mother spirit warning me. Don't fall.

The Visit   2007

How could I leave you there . . .
how kiss goodbye . . .
how cross the room . . . open the door . . .
(don't look back)
and close the door behind me,
leaving you alone . . .
Tiny, in a big blue chair.

Walking away . . . impossible
along a corridor
endless and empty . . .
your eyes bore into me
begging my return.

Irresolute . . .
turning back . . . wavering, sobbing,
I cannot do this.
I cannot see.

But there in my misted vision,
framed in an archway,
haloed in golden sparkles . . .
three figures advance towards me . . .
towards you . . . smiling.
'Is Mum all right?' one asked.

These three are part of your Star Shower,
shimmering into your room,
with their drawings . . .
and their school hats . . .
and their love.

Your Star Shower is infinite . . .
cradling you . . . enfolding you,
bobbing and shining about you . . .
There is so much love around
you will never be alone.
And that huge blue chair is growing smaller all the time.

The Promise of Easter

Hush, little one, I have your hand
even as the numbing words of death
drop in the room, across a heavy space.
And I began to remember...
The grieving slipped quietly over me
and I remembered a child I knew long ago
a girl with beautiful hair.

As quiet came the grieving
so thunderous came the demons,
banging and exploding in my head
swirling me into a spinning whirlpool of loss;
frozen in supplication,
hideous nightmare of Godless desolation.
Is this truly the cost of love?

Here the Red Queen, clip - clopping,
hooped skirt swinging,
Thrusts high on the air a myriad shining lights
weaving and soaring above and around,
spilling orbs of dazzling joy, to settle about me.
A lapful of moments, carved in time.

Now He has your hand.
You are safe. You are strong.

Fly free.

We remember Rachel with love:

We recognise her compassion as Peacemaker

We salute her courage, her patience
and fortitude

We know she loved her children and those of us
who truly loved her.

The Meek shall inherit the Earth.

We are all Individuals, each one of us a separate Being

Humankind, by and large, hunts in packs, preferring to dwell in communities, families. However, we are each our own person.

We discuss, ask advice, think carefully about the others' point of view. We ruminate, cogitate, analyse, worry. And then we make up our own minds. We all have choices . . . and we have free will.

At the end of the day we do what we do. The path we choose will not always be the right path. The decision we make will not always be without some doubt. But it is our decision.

All sorts of influences colour our judgement and the greatest of these is almost certainty love. But we have 'made our bed,' we have chosen our path and being British, Heaven help us, we do our damnedest to stick to it. But that doesn't necessarily make it right. Then we're in trouble.

Rachel had choices, like every one else. She made up her own mind, she made her bed and she did her damnedest.

In humility, however, I do ask myself whether or not the seemingly unwise choices and decisions which Rachel sometimes made, over the years, adversely affected her and possibly, due to the stress which she often suffered as a result, could have hastened or pre-empted the neurological condition which subsequently shortened her life.

Perhaps it is well that I can never possibly know.

Adapted from: For No One

> Your day breaks, your mind aches
> You find that all her words of kindness linger on
> Now she no longer needs you
> And in her eyes you see nothing
> No sign of life behind the tears, her tears.
> A love that should have lasted years.
> Your day breaks, your mind aches
> There will be time when all the things she said will fill your head.
> You won't forget her
> And in her eyes there is nothing
> No sign of life behind the tears, your tears.
> A love that should have lasted years.
>
> Lennon & McCartney 1966

Lucy in the Sky with Diamonds

Picture yourself in a boat on a river,
with tangerine trees and marmalade skies . . .
Somebody calls you, you answer quite slowly,
A girl with kaleidoscope eyes.
Cellophane flowers of yellow and green,
towering over our head.
Look for the girl with the sun in her eyes . . .
And she's gone.

Lucy in the sky with diamonds,
Follow her down to a bridge by a fountain
where rocking horse people eat marshmallow pies,
Everyone smiles as you drift past the flowers,
that grow so incredibly high.
Newspaper taxis appear on the shore,
waiting to take you away.
Climb in the back with your head in the clouds,
And you're gone.

Lucy in the sky with diamonds . . .
Picture yourself on a train in a station
with plasticine porters with looking glass ties,
Suddenly someone is there at the turnstile,
The girl with kaleidoscope eyes . . .
Lucy in the sky with diamonds . . .

Lennon & McCartney 1967

'This one is amazing. People came up and said cunningly, 'Right, I
get it . . . L S D' and it was when the Papers were talking about L S D.
But we had never thought about it. What happened was that John's
son, Julian, did a drawing at school and brought it home. He has a
schoolmate called Lucy and John said. 'What's that' and Julian said . . .
'Lucy in the sky with diamonds . . .' Paul McCartney

Confusion . . . Big Time. And then everything went black.

And then everything started to hurt, like it does, when another's pain has been acute and your own insignificant. It is true I had been hobbling a bit for a while, and that tendons and ligaments and all sorts of muscles all over the place had been in revolt . . . but I could walk. Rachel could not. She died on Easter Day '07 and by late summer Amanda took over and together with her GP in Balham, she arranged it all.

Clearly, they had ganged up on me and no protestations of mine, ('Tired? We're all tired. And No, you can sleep tomorrow,') cut any ice . . . and actually, I was too tired to fight and of course I knew they were right, which is rather a drawback in battle. So Amanda bullied me into seeing her GP, on a sort of temporary Walking Wounded basis, who, briefed and prepared for any pleas of procrastination, set about me. They do like getting at you, these Medics, don't they. Half my family is in that world which must be why I went into the Arts. Anyway I was very soon whisked, without decorum, into King's College Hospital. Here I found myself speaking somewhat incoherently, to a slightly resigned and mildly amused audience . . . the Orthopaedic Team. They were an absolute tonic after so long in the wilderness, but they weren't listening, either, to my confirmation that I was 'Fine thanks.' They simply showed me the X rays. I have to say even I was marginally impressed and so was Amanda, who never left my side. 'Ouch,' said they peering again at them. 'Bone on bone, can't do anything about that. We'll book you in . . . 4 months, get your pre ops done, oh, and do try and lose some weight. Look forward to seeing you.'

Yeah, right. I lost that one 10 - nil.

And taking up a long steel, the Consultant, with a smile in his eye, started to hone the cleaver into a dazzling silver blade. As he worked a kaleidoscope of shining precious stars fell into the room, landing at our feet.

It was, of course, a magic wand and upon its handle, carved in ivory, was an exquisite Chinese Dragon.

Part VII

The K.C.H. Experience

For Mr Li and his team

The Orthopaedic Department

Kings College Hospital

In gratitude

January 2008

O wad some Power the giftie gie us

To see oursels as ithers see us.

Robert Burns 1759 - 1796

Ships that pass in the night and

Speak each other in passing

Only a signal shown and

A distant voice in the darkness.

So on the ocean of life we pass and

Speak one another

Only a look and a voice . . .

Then darkness again and a silence.

Henry Wadsworth Longfellow 1807 – 1882

One

Visions

Silently and majestically the great ship moved slowly forward, making as she went, small ripples on the smoke black water.

Back on the quay, those who had disembarked faded like glow worms in a forest and were devoured by the night. Their journey, for the time being, was over. Whilst back on board a completely different picture was emerging.

Those who had just boarded made their way under efficient direction to their small cells, where they disrobed and climbed, some painfully, into crisp, clean, white beds already prepared to receive them.

As one, they lay back on their pillows and prepared for sleep.

* * *

Hiy Li stood alone on the bridge . . . remote and inscrutable . . . tall and imperious, wearing an elegantly cut suit. His face, chiselled and fine . . . his eyes clear and academic and his bearing at once joyful and full of purpose.

Putting his hands firmly on the rails he looked out over the sea, inky black and impenetrable. The stars were myriad and reflected fine, dancing, inviting shapes, tumbling and bouncing on the surface . . . but the moon, the moon was outstanding. A massive golden orb of mystery.

Hiy Li stretched out an arm, knowing as he always did, that he would not quite be able to reach it - to touch it. He smiled to himself - but as he kept looking up he saw quite clearly the imprint his hand had left upon the precious pearl surface. What was it about the moon that affected him so deeply? Had he been there - would he go there - could he float there?

He knew that this vision - those stars - that colossal moon were the constants of Eternity, as unshakeable as Time and as unattainable. He had always wondered about Time. It simply intrigued him.

As he turned away, smiling a little quizzical smile, he knew he was and had been part of the majesty of the scheme of all things, and he was well pleased.

Preparing to go below, he tidied his desk, scanned perfunctorily the Paper he had started to prepare, rinsed his hands, dabbed his face and dried on a fluffy white towel. He spread his hands, palms uppermost and studied them. He wondered again about the gift he had been given - the talent he could not - even had he wished - hide or neglect. John Milton, the mediaeval English poet had done just that, but then, he was forced into it by his blindness. Milton had an excuse, he however had none - and really, he was grateful for this. Why would he want to hand away something special which had been bestowed upon him? But the dream, the vision he had had so often . . . the thought of Time, of Eternity, of the Future and of the far far Past . . . his searching always touched him.

Closing the door quietly behind him he walked away, on his strange lilting gait, back into the real world . . . the world he knew . . . his world.

He ran a tight ship.

Two

Those who follow

The old lady crept painfully step by step, along the endless corridor. It reminded her of the Queen Mother when, prior to Charles and Diana's wedding, she was seen across the world, visibly to gasp as she surveyed the endless aisle of the great Cathedral, which she must process before reaching the Royal party. And of course she did it regally and with great style.

And so will this other old lady. Leaning heavily on her stick and supported by the beautiful girl who accompanied her, she plodded resolutely on.

They made a strange couple . . . the old woman bent and crooked, her face full of pain and the lithe, slim, straight-backed girl who showed such concern. Their pace slowed almost to a halt . . . they spoke no word . . . it just had to be done. While the girl, probably the daughter, inwardly remonstrated with herself for not having the foresight to arrange a wheelchair, the old woman simply made goals . . . the next corner, the next turning, where there might be a seat.

No seat appeared - what appeared was a shining angel in the form of a stunning black African lady, dressed all in white - the human garb covering the Divine. She was not small and extending herself beyond the norm, she caught up with the unlikely pair, still battling the tiles and terrazzo.

'Stay there', she commanded, 'and do not move. I will send a wheelchair for you' and she was gone.

Gratefully, the old woman clutched at the dado rail and a minute or so later, the angel reappeared, this time manhandling a dining chair.

The old woman looked at these two before her, so entirely different. The Anglo Saxon girl, tall, wafer slim, straight and confounded . . . the other statuesque, magnificently rounded, her soul shining around her in a circle of light. Both had tears in her eyes . . . the one of gratitude, the other of compassion. 'Thank you,' the fair girl said. 'Thank you so much'.

'Not at all,' replied the angel. 'Now do not move and a wheel chair will arrive very soon.' And with that she was gone, again.

That episode set the scene for the ensuing days during which the old woman would experience the composite learning, knowledge, dignity and care that science and commitment could bring to fight illness and pain.

She of course called it Love.

They were to meet again, the bent old woman and her saviour . . . in another corridor, in another place.

'How are you getting on?' the voice asked. It was the magnificent black angel, composed and smiling. She was called Toni, or Tawny, as she appropriately pronounced it.

'I am absolutely fine, thank you,' replied the old woman. (She appeared less bent - how could that be?) 'And I do want to thank you so much for saving me.'

'No really, it was nothing . . .' and she meant it.

'I however, shall never forget you,' continued the old one. The angel was visibly touched.

'That is such a nice thing to say,' she said quietly.

But it was true - in fact she would always be remembered - and in that moment she had gained some sort of added immortality, if angels have a Brownie point system.

Three

Woodstock Revisited

She was sitting grumbling to herself as the elderly frequently do - this time it was the television - it didn't work - it had eaten the money but there was no picture - all she wanted was to forget where she was and to watch some mindless rubbish.

She looked up as a figure sauntered into the room - a Dylan-esque loose limbed strolling player - a real live sixties rocker.

He . . . was . . . fabulous . . .

One is so disadvantaged sitting in a narrow bunk in a small cabin in the sick bay of a ship sailing purposefully on. What she wanted to do was point him into a comfortable chair, pour him a large brandy and discuss with him the impact of the Beatles on the social history of the Sixties and whether or not the Stones brought something far more aggressive to the pop scene of the time.

Sadly the young man had other ideas.

'My name is James,' (or was it David?) he was saying. 'I am the anaesthetist and I shall be looking after you tomorrow.'

What a put down.

He spoke in a quiet and, she thought, Irish drawl. Mercifully she didn't say as much because he went on to say he was from across the pond as he expected she had worked out. She was not sure whether or not 'Irish' is anathema to Americans. Feeling discretion the better part of valour, she kept quiet.

He rattled off a whole lot of medical gobbledegook she so much didn't want to hear, said it might be necessary to give her a blood transfusion, at which she made a face.

'W - e - l - l your haemoglobin is a bit low and we don't want any weakness.' She did manage to say 'We don't do weakness,' and he went on to ask if she had any questions, and how was she with anaesthetics?

'It was nearly forty years ago,' she said, 'and it had made me very sick indeed.'

He laughed comfortably, saying he thought things had improved a bit since then, and asked if she had anything else she wanted to ask.

Unfortunately, she thought it inappropriate to introduce the subject of the untimely death of John Lennon - its impact on the world, or to speculate on the implications of his 'Being and Becoming' had he lived.

So sadly he left her. But that had been an unexpected interlude. She realised he was another member of this amazing team, and that she was more than happy to offer up her life into his hands - for this is actually the requirement.

She knew she would see him again anyway. And so she surely did.

Four

The girl next door

Now, Sister Julie is something else.

Pretty, petite and unhurried, she moves quietly and calmly, more like 'just looking in' to a room. She has that huge gift of putting everyone at ease and is unselective in her approach.

She drops into her chair and sweeps aside the paraphernalia on her desk, although anyone with half a brain knows it is all going to come into play pretty soon.

She chats away easily and before long her victim is nodding off. But don't be fooled by the 'girl next door' illusion.

Look into her eyes. It is all there . . . Behind the merriment is her depth, her intelligence, her training, her ability and her commitment.

'Show me your hands,' she was saying.

Idiotically you spread them palms uppermost. She turns them over. Of course - she is looking for arthritis.

She chats away in a soft north country accent and we discuss regional dialects . . . whilst she slips in numerous questions. Own teeth? Any crowns? Own eyes? Any contact lenses - gentle jab - blood test.

She discusses her weekend, giggling - swab - and asks about your walking while doing your blood pressure. She stifles a gasp and offers to do it again later, indicating that the machine must be wrong . . .

You know jolly well it isn't.

Swab.

Somehow, cleverly, you find yourself on the couch behind the crown decorated blue curtains, which she closes 'because I have to.'

'I'm just going to loosen your top' she says - and groans as the horrible enormity of your black corseted torso heaves into view.

'Oh no - is this an all in one?' she nearly sighs, and is delighted to be assured it is a two piece.

'Right, good, I'm just going to listen to your chest,' and deftly whisks out her stethoscope. 'Breathe in for me,' (like you have any option) and the small steel circle wanders over your frontispiece.

'Ah, right' she says languidly. 'I'd just like a colleague to have a little listen,' and she slips away.

Convinced you are about to breathe your last, you sit bolt upright hardly noticing that your torn asunder hip doesn't actually hurt anymore, so clearly you haven't got long . . . when into the confined space steps a beautiful young man. (When you are hundreds of years old, everyone mildly younger is beautiful, and of course they are.) He had a white shirt and a very long name. He says it for you and tells you all Sri Lankan names are long - so that pins him down geographically - and with an impassive face, he thinks belies his concentration, his stethoscope follows the same course over your long suffering top as Julie's.

'No, it is fine,' he says at length. 'Bit fast, but why wouldn't it be?' replacing his steth around his neck. He agrees with your old family doctor that 'you just pump adrenaline' and smiling broadly he also slips away.

So you are not off the mortal coil then. Not quite yet.

Back comes the lovely Julie. 'Just checking.'

You are not leaving as you thought. Oh no - she hasn't quite finished.

Swab.

Rolling her clenched fist over your exposed tummy area this is where - if you are watching - you see her professionalism come into its own. All her senses are engaged. You, the person, do not exist - only your tummy - which is fair enough. Somehow, she listens and sees with her touch and her concentration is palpable.

'That's fine,' she says. 'You can get dressed.' And simultaneously your hip starts hurting again.

You are completely worn out. Julie is absolutely fine and not at all worn out.

She drops easily into her chair. You creak into yours. She writes a few notes. You crave a huge brandy.

But it's not over yet - nope.

'Just pop over there and bring me back a sample.' She hands you a weird contraption - 'and then I'll send you off for an ECG.'

And this is only the pre-med.

Oh God.

But Julie has etched a permanent little place in your heart.

Julie is great. We love her.

Five

Trees

There are no trees. Not one. Anywhere.

Just no trees.

And for someone planted long ago deep in the loam of the New Forest, this is a significant bereavement.

Of course you cannot expect trees, I suppose, given the situation.

But think about life without trees . . .

* * *

She had made her garden over the years, merging the trees she was planting with those already there.

The Ginkgo - pre history - one of the only two in the county, that had been there and was flourishing.

And the Ash - the mighty Ash up on the top lawn, waving leafy fingers at the jackdaws and the gulls.

Then there were the flowering cherries - Rowan - Holly - Yew - several old pears and fan shaped Sumac, and a three hundred year old Mulberry, slowly creaking skyward through ancient knotty joints to spread the ultimate canopy.

She had added to this abundance.

Twin Willows, whose branches last summer reached the ground.

A nut tree - a Sycamore (no it's not a weed), a Silver Birch up by the Temple, and two mighty Oaks - still only two feet tall but already protected. The latest addition is the Pittosporum. Opinion is divided as to whether this is a tree or a shrub. This one is a tree and clipped to one central trunk, it will grow to 30 feet or more.

Trees all around the lawns and the ponds.

So, there are the birds who want to eat the fish, and fish who want to eat the creatures, and seagulls who want to eat everything and who drop their babies - two every year - on to the terrace, where they finally grow, and fly, and start the procedure all over again.

* * *

And of course at the end of the lane is the sea with France only a pebble throw away. It is the Channel - not the Ocean carrying our vast ship - The Flagship of Hope.

Further west along the Jurassic Coast - beyond the Harbour - there is another ship - a prison ship - where incarcerated men await release - they have nowhere to run, only time to think. But at least some of them, the lucky ones, might, just might, be able to glimpse the stars - from their bunk in this Vessel of Despair.

* * *

But it was no good ruminating about home. She was here, in this time and there was a job to be done.

She was quite content, ambivalent even, about life . . . and death.

* * *

Note: I have included this piece again, which I wrote in 1993 because, following on from Trees, it illustrates my home environment and shows the contrast between Town and Country living, and why KCH had such a massive impact on me.

Hope . . . The Flagship . . . for Patrick Li

But then . . .
at the end of the day,
when all is said and done . . .
at the end of the lane,
past the Bunhausen row
with their scarecrow heads
and albertine wigs;
yellow in the low-glow, sun-glow, day
Dance on.

Dance past the paddock -
where in the bright of the swaying grassy floor,
a piebald and a palomino
enquire, nodding, of your kindness and your pocket.
Dance on.

Dance past the tents and the small green moving homes,
squatting in their tidy urban rows,
while in their topsy turvy roles,
fathers turn the spitting pan
upon reluctant flame
and mothers, languid, sip their Pimms . . .
Dance on.

Dance youthful, joyful, over the stile
and into the golden corn -
Look at it . . . but see it -
Touch it . . . but feel it
Know it. It holds for you a promise
It is the staff of life . . .
Dance on.

Dance up the winding
fast up the winding
throw up your arms in the clamour
of the gull-laden, scent-laden day . . .
Breathe deep, gasp, choke if you must
only live it - the blueness - the wonder.
Dance on.
Dance on. You are nearly there. Dance on.

You should stop now. Be still.
For you are come.
Place your hot hands over your eager eyes
and pray the gift of sight.
Now you may look. Look now,
and with silent humility comprehend . . . the Sea,
the Kingdom - the Power and the Glory -
For it is there. It is everywhere.
The measure of the smallness of all things.
And you have found it.
At the end of the lane...
At the end of the day.
Dance on.

Six

Mumbo Jumbo

The most amazing thing about the human spirit is its ability to adapt.

For the purpose of this piece, and as I know nothing at all, I do not intend to go too deeply into this.

But think - the Labour Camps in World War II, Terry Waite, John McCarthy, Brian Keenan, and the first men on the moon - how on earth did they all adapt? My point is far more trivial and prosaic. But we all do adapt in some way or another, to situations as they present. How we cope with bereavement for instance. The greater the loss, the greater the need - somehow - to grasp the nettle. A new school, the dentist, abuse, ageing, a new baby, divorce . . . we all adapt, and some better than others, of course.

Perhaps the usual response is

a) to go into denial or

b) to go onto another level - another plain of coping.

Perhaps it is part of Britishness, I believe it is part of Being.

* * *

'You are third on the list,' the nurse was saying briskly - 'Nil by mouth, and they will probably take you down about two. We will bring you everything you need before then - don't worry.'

She, the nurse, had done it all before, so many times.
But the old lady had not.

Right. Okay. She knew this was what she was here for. Like she knew long ago in the war there would be rationing and restrictions, partings and death - bombs and incendiaries - but nothing had really prepared her for it all actually happening. She didn't know, for instance that the terrible clattering noise coming towards her along the road was a German plane machine-gunning. How could she? She was eleven or twelve. She saw two older girls dive through a hedge and so she hid, in a handy lean to, and covered her head. She did peep behind once and saw some orange tracer bullets - but all three girls survived. They had adapted to a situation for which there are no rules.

So now, decades later, she was third on the list.

Nil by mouth - fine, she might lose a pound or two, and easily she slipped into the gown and the rather pretty little paper pants which the nurse cheerfully gave her.

And then she sat on her bed and waited.

Worried? No. Frightened? Not really. Hardly the trenches, but she had adapted to this situation. She had gone onto another level - a kind of conscious unconsciousness - alert and accepting - she knew where she was - why she was there - she knew and implicitly trusted her team. She was fine, sort of.
She was fine.

She also knew that life is finite and this might be her final exiat, perhaps she was about to embark on the journey of the soul - further to experience the line of Time upon which she believed absolutely that humankind progress along. This was not a religious concept necessarily - it was simply the conviction of a free spirit, hatched and immersed in the heart of the green earth - of the natural progression and economy of life and what we call death. She had watched the world around her regenerate itself year after year. Why would not the mind, the intelligence, the consciousness, go forward? Attribute it where you will. The Universe - The Creator - The Prophet - Buddha - Jesus Christ - the Great Juju - it doesn't matter - in the end we are all part of the scheme of things; part of the Infinite - part of Time.

(This homespun philosophy, for me, clearly shows the futility of War and entirely negates the fear of Death.)

She would like to have gone on arguing with herself - but actually, together with a nurse, she was being whisked at great speed along endless corridors . . . down . . . down in the lift, more corridors, more lifts, less people - and no windows. Scary.

It seemed to her that she was being transported - by a very cheerful chap in a grey uniform - rather like a tracksuit - down into the very bowels of the earth. Far away - far from all that was familiar.

Actually, of course, the speedy journey came to an abrupt end.

She was in the Holding Bay . . .

Seven

The Holding Bay

Although there was an air of quiet expectancy - all was silent in the seriously weird and huge space. Obviously we were in the foundations of the building - grey and massive - rather like an air raid shelter, but big enough to be a bunker under the War Office. A few crayoned pictures peered down pathetically from the walls, probably provided by local schoolchildren.

Trolleys lined up around the walls inhabited by silent bodies, all pretty ancient, like our old lady . . . All except one young man who had clearly damaged his arm or shoulder. The faces were completely impassive - they had all adapted to their situation and had gone into a sleepy withdrawal.

Needless to say, even in this strange space there was a light. From out of a corner - decorated by endless files and lists and the odd photo thrown in, stepped a busy little lady. She was not young - about four feet tall - and she was of course an absolute gem. Clearly in command of her assignment (she had probably done the job for years) she whisked around the trolleys with her files.

The nurse stood patiently beside the trolley bearing the old lady. Her name was Shanti Jung, I think, and she was an Indian princess. She had the beauty of her race. Lovely dark hair and large, limpid doe eyes full of mystery. She had a remote Mona Lisa quality and endless patience. She stayed long enough for both the gladsome lady and another check maker to trawl through their notes, and then she left. The checks were precisely the same in both cases - she knew the routine well. Name, date of birth, (it was still fairly clear that the old one was female) and did she have a mark on her leg. One of the checkers said, 'can I see it, please?' and obediently was shown the mauve marker arrow, which travelled north and explicitly stated HIP! These constant checks have to be applauded. From the word go there was never the slightest chance that the wrong hip was going to be assaulted. The old girl was well content, lay back on her pillow and thought of nothing at all. She was soon out of the Holding Bay, into the next stage . . . and counting . . .

Eight

Nearing The End. Which End? AHA!

The long and winding road was reaching its conclusion. Somehow she was in another room - and there was the strolling player - looking very focussed and wearing something really hip on his head - a kind of tea cosy - but actually a rather splendid striped kerchief, tied at the back.

With him was a splendid young doctor who advanced upon her and started to talk about Jags. This was right up the old girl's street and she responded enthusiastically, giving him details of her first Jag back in the '60's. An XKI20 - wire wheels - rag top - and the power of a rocket. In retrospect he might have said JAB referring to the jab he was about to put into her wrist when he could find a suitable vein. He was kind and joined into the discussion of Jaguar cars, and feigned a suitable interest, whilst he set about her with a hypodermic.

Blood spurted like a fountain, she was rather proud of the quantity - she should really think about giving blood - when from behind the trolley advanced Bob Dylan, in real, proper anaesthetist mode, and very scary.

'What are you doing?' he boomed, in a 'not to be trifled with' stage whisper - mopping the blood from the trolley, the cover, her hand. She was very impressed with it all but slunk deeper into her pillow and for once in her life kept quiet. She did give a fleeting thought to the night before when he had said 'you might need a blood transfusion' - but knowing that you can't put blood back into a stone, or a vein, she remained silent.

All was serene in a very few minutes when, complete with endless inlets and outlets, the glorious one asked her to sit on the edge of the trolley - put a pillow on her lap and made a bit of small talk while the young doctor did something skillful with a size eight rawl plug in her back.

Question - why did he put a pillow on her lap?

She was calm and perfectly happy with the people she had grown to trust.

She knew no more . . . .

* * *

. . . . which was a shame really, since she had wondered the night before in the dark hours whether she could manipulate an 'out of body experience' so that she could observe her wonderful team, in its entirety, working with precision on the job in hand.

Why would they bother? An obstreperous old woman in a more or less spent body.

They bothered, of course, because this is what they did, regardless of age or of anything else. They were and are committed to preserving life in as comfortable a state as all their collective skill and learning can achieve.

And I applaud them.

Nine

One for the Shrink

No out of body experience then - that was a shame - perhaps she never quite reached the 'near death' point.

Her eyelids fluttered, and what she saw made her close them again very quickly while she considered her situation. In one sweep she had taken in an extraordinarily long room - empty trolleys lining the walls in serried rows, each with a Doctor Who type contraption looming large beside and above. But the thing which really threw her - in this one glance - was a female figure standing nearby. She was saying 'She's coming round' to another female figure - who looked precisely the same in every detail - same height - same look - same uniform - same black shiny hair trimmed into a short bob. Quite clearly they were clones and obviously part of some Mafia.

And now the old lady had somehow to cope with this. She decided at once that the best thing was to stay inert as long as possible with eyes tight shut - and to go along with the pantomime. If they were to transport her somewhere weird then she must counteract by using her brain. She would just go along with it, whatever came. They were speaking to each other, these girl clones, and while they were thus occupied, the old girl took another crafty look around her . . . She had never in her life seen such a room. It was so HUGE, so LONG - 60 feet - 60 yards - more? Or was it all done with mirrors - like the use of a mirror in a painting that reflects the same painting in the mirror - time and time again - into infinity. The method has a name, is it trompe l'oeil? Anyway, the room either was, or was not, vastly long. She was mildly encouraged to see the young man with the damaged arm lying unconscious a few trolleys down. Oh. So he was off as well then. If she were in a parallel Universe - then clearly he was too - so that was a slight comfort.

All was grey and out of focus - silent and sweet smelling - the room, the trolleys, the clone girls came and went from her vision - in a sensation of drifting - she couldn't see very well and that too was a comfort.

However, she was not to rest on her laurels for long because soon she was actually being transported by an unseen figure with a far away voice, along the corridors and in the lifts she thought she had traversed before. The same, but not the same. She kept very still - while she assessed the situation - she saw the pictures and posters on the walls. The pictures were similar to those on the downward journey, but they were not the same - not exact, not the ones. Those had been sharply defined and densely coloured. These were not. These were shadowy images.

The trolley jerked left into a small cabin, not unlike the one she had been occupying before - but not the same - smaller and mistier. They had arranged similar furniture around the room, and even on the table the photograph of her grand daughter looked almost the same - but it was not. It had obviously been put through a copier many times and was therefore dull and hazy.

Oh but they were clever - these aliens.

'We are just going to put you onto your own bed,' the voice said. They made her comfortable and departed. She did not actually see who spoke.

And there on the wall opposite her bunk was the picture. So clever and suddenly so horrible. The same tulips . . . Solomon's seal . . . Euphorbia - yet not at all the same.

From out of the dark loam at the base of the plants stepped forth weird creatures, and above, peering through the stems of the once beautiful tulips, were alien faces with saucer eyes - unlike anything she had seen before . . . and they were beckoning.

She knew in her brain that they were not real, but they - it all - was looking pretty convincing. Then quite suddenly she realised the pain had gone.

The grinding pain that she had lived with for so long. So perhaps she had died and gone . . . where? Obviously into a parallel Universe.

She needed her kids: if she had gone to this alien place, it would be nice to know that they were also part of it. The key point was she knew that she could trust them . . . implicitly. And there they were, laden with cakes and biscuits and chocolates - 'Sorry darling, flowers not allowed, infection dontchuknow . . .'

They were all happy - the old girl was high. The conversation got louder and louder until a nurse told the old woman she 'must calm down.'

The grand daughter said she was not at all phased by all the drips and the masks and stuff. She had 'seen it all before on Holby,' whatever that meant.

And they left - all was quiet and dark.

The old woman slept.

Ten

Conclusion

And that's about it, really.

She was sorry that she did not know the names of so many of the people who had helped so much during her stay.

The cleaners in grey who wielded brushed and dusters constantly – who leaned on their brooms for a small chat about life.

The cooks in blue who produced meals all the time and who danced into her room full of good cheer.

The dozens of nurses who came in shifts - she listened to them all.

She would probably never know now whether Sister Nora is pregnant with this much wanted baby.

The sado-masochist physios who taught her how to walk and insisted that she did so.

The boy nurse from the Philippines with whom she discussed the Tsunami - 'In the islands,' he said, 'we knew about the weather but we didn't have the wave.'

The Sister who came into the country girl's room, where the windows were open, an unusual sight - she who fled at once and commanded the nurse from the Philippines to 'go in and close the windows, she's (the old woman) freezing to death in there.' The country girl wasn't, the Sister was . . . The windows stayed closed for an hour or so.

The various people who came in and out discussing pain relief - and the ward rounds, they were great fun - the only thing was they took place at 8 a.m . . . quite uncivilised. So she never really got into her stride.

The lovely doctor with the wonderful dark hair, smiling eyes and a great sense of the ridiculous, led in the team one morning. She told him she had wanted to have, or at least have sight of, her damaged part - which they had replaced, and where was it? He laughed and asked why on earth she had wanted it? And she replied that she had wanted to put it under her pillow for the Tooth Fairy. He and the team all chortled, the joke was a hit but she didn't get the offending article. A couple of days later he came back when she was dying in her bunk. 'How are you?' he asked - 'Terrible, thank you,' she whispered - she was not joking. 'Take her off the Diclofenac,' he said to the sister, and from that moment she started to recover. She loved him and lived.

And then there was Chakrabarti - she would never forget him or his cool name - and was he anything to do with Reeta of the same name? Radio 4, Sunday nights, The Westminster Hour?

She supposed she would never know any of these things, unless they would have her back to do the other hip.

James, or was it David, the rocking anaesthetist, had said - 'Come back in a couple of months, we'll do the other one.'

Kind, and a good offer -

She smiled and said nothing -

She thought 'I don't think so.'

But all in all it was a tremendous experience and although she would not give up her life in darkest Dorset, she wouldn't have missed it for anything.

She was pain free - she was cared for and she was more than grateful. There are two more people who have, throughout, been a huge part of this exercise.

One is Dr Ribiero in Balham Health Centre, who in the months available before the op gave her the most extensive M.O.T so that all was as well as it could be, and not too many surprises at the time of the pre-assessment. He did a marvellous job, performing every test in the book – took arms full of blood and looked alarmed and happy in turn. Generally speaking, all was well, and anything which was not, he treated. He deserves, and has, my gratitude.

Similarly, the post-op tests, all done and all seems to be well. We saw him often and he gave his time and diligence. And sometimes, not often, we made him smile.

The other person is of course my daughter Amanda - who having bullied me unmercifully for a long time . . . 'for heaven's sake get your hip done' . . . finally arranged for the whole episode to take place in London. She and Dr Ribiero chose KCH from his list (close to home, a teaching hospital and a great reputation) and it went on from there . . . irrevocably.

Amanda did it all. The endless phone calls. All my records were lost in the mists of time and had to be dug up from Ferndown, in Dorset. The only number I had was my identity card number (war time) EEOM1145. Dr Ribiero sighed, and said 'too early.'

Eventually the NHS and NI Nos. were located - but nothing was easy or straightforward - but together with a network of people, who each contributed something, the job was set in motion.

Amanda and her daughter Lily gave their time, their home and in Amanda's case - her timetable - her income - her life, in the setting up, the execution and the aftercare required for this entire project. Her house is given over to aids for the elderly and disabled, and rooms adapted and made into no go areas.

So much outside and beyond the call of filial duty - (oh, and the son fell in with a necessary injection of cash to help the dwindling finances.)

This has been a transparent display of love. It cannot have been easy to have a crabby old woman invading her/their space - but it has been achieved in the spirit of giving . . . and never a cross word.

She deserves and has my loving thanks.

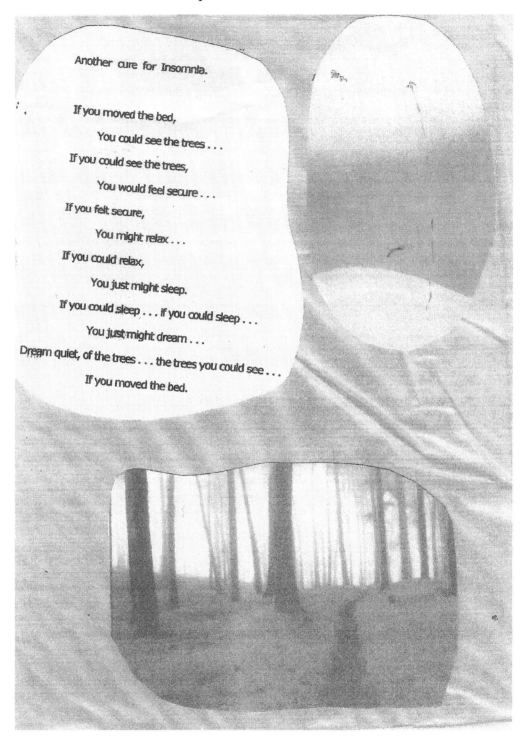

Another cure for Insomnia.

If you moved the bed,

You could see the trees . . .

If you could see the trees,

You would feel secure . . .

If you felt secure,

You might relax . . .

If you could relax,

You just might sleep.

If you could sleep . . . if you could sleep . . .

You just might dream . . .

Dream quiet, of the trees . . . the trees you could see . . .

If you moved the bed.

Another Day at K. C. H

'Six months,' you said, or a year?'
We went into shock - the child and I
For once silenced . . . unusual.
Six months, you said.

Six months or a year . . .
So long - so different -
Squinting, owl - like,
Through the long defective eye of age.
Of extreme age.
Presupposes so much,
Assumes so much.
How can we know -
The child and I?
We cannot know . . .
A day may be too long.

And yet we did it
And all remains the same.
People like ants - swarming -
Up down and over -
Doctors busy with clipboards,
Nurses fussing with lists -
All except Jules, who deserted in the name of Love.

But there, in a bubble of inherent, cultural calm
Mr Li - and only twelve more clients today.
Clever that. Quite right.
And there's another accolade,
More gold braid.
Quite right.
And soon we shall call you Sir.

But to us -
The child and me
You are, and will always be . . .
Li Li - Glorious
The Glorious God of Bone.
Quite right.

Part VIII

Amanda

How do I love Thee . . .

How do I love thee? Let me count the ways . . .
I love thee to the depth and breadth and height
My soul can reach, when feeling out of sight . . .
For the ends of Being and ideal Grace.
I love thee to the level of every day's
Most quiet need by sun and candlelight.
I love thee freely, as men strive for Right;
I love thee purely, as they turn from Praise.
I love thee with the passion put to use
In my old griefs, and with my childhood's faith.
I love thee with a love I seemed to lose
With my lost saints . . . I love thee with the breath,
Smiles, tears of all my life . . . and if God choose
I shall but love thee better after death.

'Yes,' I answered you last night;
'No', this morning, Sir I say.
Colours seen by candlelight
Will not look the same by day.

The Lady's Yes . . .

I tell you, hopeless grief is passionless.

Sonnets. Grief.

Elizabeth Barrett - Browning. 1806 – 1861

Look, Mummy, no hands!

Speaking of Amanda, which we were, or if we were not at that moment, we soon would have been . . . What can I say and where can I possibly start?

Why not with her 40th birthday, that's as good a place as any. Except it leaves so much that went before, unsaid. Party lights, party mood, party people and of course a whopping great cake and hundreds of candles. Well 40, anyway.

And good will and happiness abounding.

'And now, at the risk of embarrassing Amanda and boring the rest of you,' said the voice, 'I just for a moment want to tell you about my daughter. Daughters are a delightful and invariably expensive commodity. They will borrow your most precious belongings and your last pound note, which in spite of fervent promises, you will never see again. They will laugh with you and weep with you . . . they will tell you, 'You CAN'T wear that Mummy,' when you think you've made a pretty good job of your Speech Day rig out . . . they will raise your blood pressure and lower your bank balance and just when you think it's all going rather well, they can be relied upon to come up with another disaster far more awful than the last.

Daughters, therefore, are pretty dreadful on the whole and I promise you, my daughter is and has been, no less ghastly than everyone else's . . .

But expendable they aint.

And they are so clever.

Practically from the moment of birth, when they clench their fists and go blue in the face and say they will choke if you don't pick them up, the die is cast . . . as with great skill and progressive dexterity, they proceed to fashion YOUR future.

As parents we are a doomed race; it is our children who do the rearing.

Amanda is a child of the spin off from the Sixties. That is when she learned to 'let it all hang out', whatever that might mean and when she was frequently sent home for abandoning her school uniform in favour of a cassock and a psychedelic overshirt. No doubt the elderly of Street benefitted from her imposed punitive care.

The Beatles were singing 'All you need is Love'. I agreed with them then. I agree with them still. And so does Amanda. They were great days.

But Amanda is growed up now.

Like all families, we have had our disasters . . . not least of them is that cake . . . Disasters cannot be avoided.

We have had our breakdowns and our broken hearts, it's par for the course, but throughout it all Amanda's love has never wavered. She, like all of you, has been there . . . with support and humour and common sense. It is a two way oneness. And I thank her for all those years of love.

Amanda has many guises and many names . . . So Mandy, Minochka, Amanda or Min . . .

Let's slice the cake and merry make and ask, what's in a name?

Enjoy your next 40 years, darling . . .'

Sob.

Bank Manager's Lament

The Arty Client

I'm here, I think
drowning in the dross of yesterday's happenings
impedimenta of another time,
dead sagging glitz - still throbbing.

My head hurts
my tongue fills my being
splurging from my ears and nose
like ectoplasm -
And you talk to me of pence.

Pence darling, do not do this -
Speak to me of Byron, of el Seraglio
of Hogarth, acanthus or of Monet's calm
And trust tomorrow's dream.

Soon now, my wondrous file,
the constant cause of anguish to your noble arse
mounted in roses - pops tinkling up
no longer coloured red
and bells will ring -
Trust me, I'm an artist.

But you are valued - yes!
And I shall feed you grapes
in clouds of dollar printed gauze -
For if I could either see my feet or feel them,
there would you be, gently caressing them
and, with golden pins,
firmly hammering them to the floor!

Oh, and have you got change for the phone?

Damsel in Distress

Last night I saw your death
putty skin, stretched like an old lampshade
over ugly twisted bones.
Your eyes, once beautiful, sunk away
buried in hollow bruise - black circles
open, lifeless on a marble slab
focusing beyond nowhere . . .
Your mouth displaced into a twisted nothing.

And then your voice,
from far off anonymity, choked and sweetly said,
'I was just thinking . . .'

Today, the miracle of resurrection
pale jigsaw face put back together –
reassembled somehow into Venus form
gulping in life - acknowledging the damage.
Two steps slowly forward - one step back –
The gift of one more day.

TO BE HAPPY FOR AN HOUR

GET DRUNK

TO BE HAPPY FOR A YEAR

FALL IN LOVE

TO BE HAPPY FOR LIFE

TAKE UP GARDENING   Chinese Proverb

The Gardener

The man who does the garden
is a lovely sort of man:
with arms all strong and hairy
and a face all over tan.
He's an awful friend of mine,
and when I'm bigger, if I can,
I'll just be like the man who does the garden.

Big men don't fuss with hankies,
they just sniff and use their hand . . .
and when I'm big enough to do
just what I like, I've planned,
I'll never wash, nor brush my hair,
nor clean my toosies . . .
AND I shall SPIT,
like the man who does the garden!   Anon 1945

The Glory of the Garden

Our England is a garden; and such gardens are not made
By singing 'Oh how beautiful', and sitting in the shade.
So when your back stops aching and your hands begin to harden,
You can call yourself a partner in the Glory of the Garden.

Borrowed from Rudyard Kipling 1911

Going forth . . . in Love

All that was some time ago and in the ensuing years Amanda, like everyone else, had her ups and downs.

She made an unfortunate marriage. But she has a most wonderful daughter called Lily. These two are my constant joy and the light of my life. They live far off in the Land of London, but we are in touch on a more or less daily basis and we push each other around in the pram of life and get along against the odds, somehow or other.

The story of Min's being a lone parent is too harrowing and too prolonged to go into here . . . and anyway, that is her story and I hope she will write that best seller in the fullness of time. Suffice it is to say that she is a fantastic mother and has brought Lily up to be the whole person that she is. They are loving and caring, not only for each other but for everyone who comes into their orbit and for many who do not. Lily, now17, is in her final year of sixth form and is a loved and respected member of the school.

Amanda has had her 50th birthday, which is quite ridiculous as she is the original Petra Pan. She is a professional gardener and is the happiest and most positive of creatures. She recently had a T.V. Programme called Digging Deep, which was both charming and gruelling to watch, since it portrayed precisely what it was that the title indicated. Sadly we now have the Economic Downturn which has put paid to a further series, for the time being at any rate.

She also has an allegorical book presently out doing the publishers, but never an easy market to break into, that area has also been hit by the economy and so is taking its time.

Amanda however has an irrefutable belief in all things happening for a reason, and that God and the Universe will turn things around and all will become clear and good. I only hope she is right.

I have written so many pieces for Amanda over the years . . . funny, sad, worrying, encouraging and so on . . . I shall include a few and perhaps they will illustrate, in some measure, her astounding attitude.

Amanda

She has the ability and the know - how
She has the inner strength and the energy,
But above all, she has the eye.
She can see outside and beyond,
She can see what others cannot perceive,
She can see the finished article.

She will give all her time, all her sleeping hours
and all her emotion.
Whatever she is asked to do, she will consider
 . . . very carefully.
If she takes it on, she will deliver.

All you have to do is:
Give her her head,
Give her time,
Leave her alone . . .
And above all . . .
Trust her.

And every now and again,
when you see the signs. you need to say,
'Amanda, stop.'

The Journey . . . for Amanda

I see you standing straight and tall, taller, taller,
golden sand between your toes
sunlight whisping golden hair
and the ocean lapping, lapping.

Transfixed, I watch you gently circle,
not a Dervish whirling, whirling,
graceful swaying, Fonteyn spinning,
Fonteyn spinning, spinning.

And as you slowly spin
arms extended, higher, higher,
palms upturn, beseeching
submissive and beseeching.

Strange loosening as ephemera
drops from your Rackham gauze
lets go, unhands resisting folds
dripping, dropping.

Slow the spinning stops . . .
Light, radiant you unfold
to the music of the playful waves
lapping, lapping.

Penitent inside the circle
meaningless and useless dross,
teardrops will dissolve the hurting
falling, falling.

In Grace you step, high kicking
from that circle into the next
take a small hand, sweetly proffered
waiting, loving.

I see you liberated, free
into the new dawn glowing,
I see your compassion and your joy . . .
Happy . . . Happy.

For Amanda, Cracking Up in France.

Hush little one, it's quiet now
The eye of the hurricane, shattering in its approach
has passed.
You are up . . . you are alive . . . walk on.

Stretch long
Stretch your limbs up into the yellow sunlight
and shake your mane with even a querulous snort.

Breathe deep
Breathe in the newness of a fresh and dewy era
And listen to your mind.

The mind is the shrine of your own thinking
it belongs to you alone.
Reject from your mind the trivia
which, like goblins in the night
insidiously invades the importance of perennial priority.
Analyse and enquire
and from the cinders of the incinerated whole,
clutch gropingly at those small green blades
which, because of their insistence
qualify, and deserve another scrutiny.

And now, the brain knocks bossily at the door of the mind.
The brain, custodian of your conviction
applies its logic, its reason and its truth,
the thesis of the aggregate of your belief.
An homogenous whip of open minded sense.
The tight rope of reality.

But the heart, Amanda, ah the heart
The haven of your resolve
carries on its crest, the total sum of mind and brain
stirred liberally with emotion.
The poetry of fantasy.

Safe within the armour of the brain,
bearing high the Colour of the mind,
the heart will lead you unafraid
into the realms of giving
in the knowledge
that the price of giving is acceptance
and acceptance is the fullness;
the gift of the whole person.

Joanie   Little Min

You'll never walk alone

When you walk through a storm
Hold your head up high
And don't be afraid of the dark

At the end of the storm
Is a golden sky
And the sweet silver song of the lark

Walk on through the wind
Walk on through the rain
Though your dreams be tossed and blown

Walk on walk on with hope in your heart
And you'll never walk alone
You'll never walk alone

When you walk through a storm
Hold your head up high
And don't be afraid of the dark

At the end of the storm
Is a golden sky
And the sweet silver song of the lark

Walk on through the wind
Walk on through the rain
Though your dreams be tossed and blown

Walk on walk on with hope in your heart
And you'll never walk alone
You'll never walk

You'll never walk
You'll never walk alone.

Rodgers & Hammerstein 1945

Part IX

THE ECHO CARDIOGRAM 'Ah yes . . . A.F . . . Thought so . . .'

THE 24 HOUR MONITOR

ECG . . . ECG . . . ECG . . . ECG . . . >>> . . . ad infinitum

Two Thousand and Ten A.D . . .

Slipped quietly into place . . . on the domestic front at any rate. War was raging around the world, with Iraq and Afghanistan the main focus. 'You have to watch the Middle East,' my mother had said when I was about ten years old. 'It is, and always has been, a hot bed of war and revolution.' I'm not sure what I was meant to do about it - then - or now - except I worry now. I didn't then.

Christmas had passed and New Year's Eve came and went. I spent it, as always, in bed with Jools Holland. By Amanda's birthday at the end of January, we were in the grip of a deep freeze and my heating died. Minus 4 degrees in my bedroom . . . and heating kaput. I don't feel the cold particularly . . . I just found a few extra blankets. But something did - and what turned out to be my heart, actually shivered, loudly. This caused panic stations at King's College Hospital on the 4th of February, when I went up for a routine pre-assessment prior to my left THR. The lovely Sister looked a bit phased when I told her of the hypothermia incident. 'First of all you can't call it hypothermia. It wasn't diagnosed. And it sounds cardiac to me,' she said cheerfully and after a swift chat with the anaesthetist, it was all systems go . . . In came the Big Guns. ECG - 24hr monitor - Echo Cardiogram . . . 'A F'. Hmm. Thought so,' they said. Anyway, that seemed all right and 'On with the Motley'. . . . Nearly there. It's good sometimes, to be a layman.

On the 14th May the Glorious God of Bone performed the magic. The operation was a complete success and all was very well. Now I had two new hips. What a privilege to be part of this great country and to have access to such care. After the six week period, I returned to KCH for X ray and discharge. Testament to the attention offered and received in that wonderful Teaching Hospital and, of course, the love and help I was given by Dr. Ribiero and Amanda and Lily I was free to go . . . free soon, to make my way back to my beloved Dorset.

And that should have been the end. But it was not. Oh no.

I said unto the man who stood at the Gate of the Year . . .

'Give me a light that I may tread safely into the unknown'

And he replied

'Go out into the darkness

And put your hand into the hand of God

That shall be better to you than light . . .

And safer than a known way.'

Minnie Louise Haskins 1939.
Christmas speech George VI
Queen Elizabeth, the Queen Mother, loved this piece and
gave it to George VI who used it as above.

Hip Popping

Once there was a hip who thought he was a dancer,
But he knew it couldn't last,
He turned out to simply be chancer
So we put him in the past . . .
Get back . . . Get back . . . Get back to where you once belonged,
Get back . . . Get back . . . Get back to where you once belonged.
GET BACK HIP

Adulteration of 'Get Back.'

Beatles Roller Coaster song 1969

It was just the beginning of the Hip Popping Period.

Between June and the end of August I popped it out 4 times, each time more scary and more painful than the last. It's called Subluxation, and no, I don't want to know that either.

I'm sure it was always my fault, something I did or didn't do . . . however aware I was, however stressed Amanda and I became, take your eye off the ball for one moment and POP. There we go again. Oh NO. Help.

The Glorious God of Bone saw me several times and rigorously took me through all the do's and don'ts, sometimes with actions. He arranged for Physio in Dorset and gradually my confidence returned. By my next appointment at KCH I had got through 3 months . . . 13 weeks . . . 91 days of muscle building - hip popping free.

How good was that. Smiley Face.

G of B was visibly thankful, saying 'whatever you are doing is right . . . carry on . . . and come and see me again in three months.'

Right Ho.

Great . . . Smiley Face.

And put another way . . .

I want to say my thankyous
For all your care and time
Afraid to tempt the Fates, cos I'm
Completely paranoid.

I've listed all the do-s and don't-s
Impaled them on my moind
I do it all, just once forget . . . POP!
That's why I'm paranoid.

I've found again the book of words,
I've learned it all by rote,
I could just try it gently, but
Not yet, I'm paranoid.

'There's a swivel thing, put on your seat,
It'll take the weight' they say . . . or
'Get a monkey pole . . . try roller skates . . .'
I'm not THAT paranoid.

The Elfin one subdued a tear
and squared up at my side,
'We can do it. Here drink this,
And don't be paranoid.'

The God of Bone said, 'Try a shower,'
The son said, 'Great, I'll pay,'
They neither know how much they ask
of me, I'm paranoid.

Said Chakrabati 'Lose some weight.'
Ribiero said the same . . .
But whichever way I look at it
I just don't like this game.

I want to float on gossamer,
Step weightless on the moon,
Or be a Jackdaw in the Ash, just
Not me, I'm paranoid.

I'll do it all tomorrow,
Head high, hip well in place,
And when tomorrow is today,
I won't be paranoid.

Warning (Staccato)

90 Degrees
90 Degrees
Don't lean over
Bend your knees
Watch your angle
Choose your chair
Op foot forward
Take great care
When you drop it
Use a grabber
Or better still
Just leave it there.

Op leg backward
That's the angle
Now just slightly
Bend your trunk
When you're standing
Use a plum line
Nose to toe
Each every time.
In and out of bed is harder
And the car, impossible
My advice, in both these cases
Close your eyes and
Take a pill.

ANDWHATEVERYOUDODONTONANYACCOUNTTWIST
COSIFYOUDOYOUREALLYWILLREGRETITIFYOULIVE
THATIS.FORGETTHEBEATLESTWISTANDSHOUT.LISTEN
IAMWARNINGYOUIFYOUDOYOUWILL.YOUREALLYWILLAND
ITSNOTAPRETTY SIGHT.

Oh good, that's got that off my chest then.

173

Keep Calm and Carry On

While all this was going on, there was life outside and beyond the Hip. Amanda got a job in Design, Lily had her 18th Birthday and sat her A Levels, with good and happy results, Hermione waltzed into Oxford with 10 A Stars and Steve took his O Levels also with good results. So that was all wonderful.

Within the larger circle of friends and family there were some joyful births and sadly some departures.

Around the world wars were still raging - and our Serving Boys started coming home badly wounded and some, of course, had died. Politics staggered on - both sides right and both sides of course, wrong. With usual fickleness, big names came and went with little or no comment on the world situation, nor noticeable effect.

However, having been given a clean bill of health, I was travelling serenely, on November 23rd back to my beloved Dorset.

Thanks be to God and to the God of Bone and the fantastic Ortho team at KCH.

10 miles east of Stonehenge, however, at the Countess roundabout, the balloon went up. The driver behind hurtled into the back of me - writing off my beloved Jag and wrecking my body. Two days later my left hip dislocated. You don't want to do that. Ever.

The accident took me back to square one but in a far worse condition than prior to the hip replacement in May. I was completely devastated and although the hip had been manipulated in Dorchester it had been rendered unstable by the accident. So on December 2nd I was back in Mr Li's consulting room. He was shocked to see me again so soon . . . as were the staff when I turned up – this time in a wheel chair. Yet another operation was planned, to replace the replacement.

'Life is what happens to you while you're busy making other plans.'

Despair

I am groping through cobwebs
torn by cobweb blades and bleeding -
not the tinsel kind draped dewy
on a hedgerow.
I'm talking menace here.

Worse far than rat infested cellar
worse, much worse, than Havisham despair
for her lost love.
Those were theirs.
I'm talking black here.

Dense glutinous shrouds reach out
embracing me . . .
No light anywhere
No light. None.
I'm talking threatening here.

Moving forward into it
Searching for beyond - which cannot be,
Since forward might be back
and beyond behind . . .
I'm talking nightmare here.

Get . . . these . . . things . . . off . . . me
Tear them from my eyes
Drag them from my tangled hair
and thus encapsulate the hands, the arms
and in a sudden sludge-grey swirl
Mummify the whole person.

And so it goes
Oh God, help me
It's all too much . . . I've had enough
I'm out of here.
I'm talking seriously done for . . .
Switch . . . on . . . the . . . light.

I'm down . . .

I'm down, (I'm really down)

I'm down. (Down on the ground)

I'm Down, I'm really down . . .

How can you laugh when you know I'm down.

(How can you laugh?)

Man buys ring, woman throws it away,

Same old thing happens every day,

I'm down, (I'm really down)

I'm down - down on the ground

I'm down - I'm really down . . .

How can you laugh, when you know I'm down?

How can you laugh?

We're all alone and there's nobody else,

You still say 'Keep your hands to yourself',

I'm down, I'm really down

I'm down, down on the ground.

How can you laugh, when you know I'm down.

How can you laugh?

Oh yeah . . .

Lennon & McCartney 1965

You need Help

I'm down. Yeah thanks John and Paul. I do so get that. Always have. But in more than 40 years I've done it, seen it, eaten it and read it. (Forget the T shirt darling, so unbecoming.)

And my girls dance Down - graphically, amusingly, convincingly and with tremendous verve. They can do Down.

I know about Down. I do Down extremely efficiently . . . and this time I reckon I've done Down to death. Yeah, I know you can't measure Down. One man's Down is another man's pecking a crumb off a bird table . . . but each man's Down, to him, is paramount.

Down comes in many forms.
Down is Pain . . . I'm talking agony here.
Down is seething with resentment and therefore more pain.
Down is shock. . . . an uncomprehending and uncontrollable dive into a morass of slithery black goo.
Down is a gradual seeping away of strength, of conviction, of will, of the You that makes you You.
Oh yes, Sunshine, you're Down!

You don't need Insurance Companies and Solicitors dragging up, over and over again, (for your own good, you understand,) the last miniscule bit of information about the accident you have had, and because you yourself are cynical and generally nasty, you also know that every phone call, every letter, every email that lands up on your desk, effectively swells their bulging coffers. Theirs, note, not yours.

So over a long period of time, seven plus months (two years and three months at the time of this edit,) you are required to vomit up and to relive the horror that put you into this situation.

So, actually it's exactly what you don't need for your recovery. It's not Rocket Science. You need Help!

But help is always just around the corner, waiting for you to open the door.

You better believe it. Hang in there.

Help!

Help, I need somebody,
Help, not just anybody,
Help, you know I need someone, help.

When I was younger, so much younger than today,
I never needed anybody's help in any way.
But now these days are gone, I'm not so self assured,
Now I find I've changed my mind and opened up the doors.

Help me if you can, I'm feeling down
And I do appreciate you being round.
Help me, get my feet back on the ground,
Won't you please, please help me.

And now my life has changed in oh so many ways,
My independence seems to vanish in the haze.
But every now and then I feel so insecure,
I know that I just need you like I've never done before.

Help me if you can, I'm feeling down
And I do appreciate you being round.
Help me, get my feet back on the ground,
Won't you please, please help me.

When I was younger, so much younger than today,
I never needed anybody's help in any way.
But now these days are gone, I'm not so self assured,
Now I find I've changed my mind and opened up the doors.

Help me if you can, I'm feeling down
and I do appreciate you being round.
Help me, get my feet back on the ground,
Won't you please, please help me, help me, help me, oh.

Lennon & McCartney 1965

All the world's a stage . . .

and all the men and women merely players.
They have their exits and their entrances,
and one man in his time plays many parts,
his acts being seven ages . . . . . .

Shakespeare. 'As you like it.'

And as I was saying . . .

Help is always just around the corner, you have to be aware and let help find you.

Enter Miracle Man

Kevin Turner walks in the light.

A strange thing to say about someone you barely know, have only recently met and then only professionally. I don't know his date of birth, his life style or his taste in music.

But I repeat - Kevin Turner walks in the light.

He arrived in a clapped out old car, carrying a sort of modern Doctor's bag and with a quiet grace. He came almost unbidden, following an altercation with my Insurance Company. They had offered me, (nay insisted upon) a course of physio arranged by them. Failure to accept their guy would result in my having to foot the entire bill from the accident and probably being burned at the stake. A red rag to any passing bull and one I refused coldly, saying I already had an extremely good Physio, thank you, with whom I was very happy and suggested they might like to take a running jump. They won, of course, as they invariably do, having time always to grind the client into the proverbial.

It turned out that the Physio Duo had trained together and knew and respected each other. Everybody thought everything was fine, except me. I sulked rather. I was having a dose of PTSD at the time, so I was allowed to sulk.

Kevin Turner was the Physio of course. He arrived in a clapped out old car. He accepted, almost eagerly, a cup of coffee which I offered, mildly grudgingly and he proceeded to fill in the required forms and particulars. He was simply doing his job.

He quickly knew all the reasons for his being there, his questioning cogent, appropriate and humorous. He so didn't care and I liked that.

Almost against my will I started to warm to this great Bear of a young man. Entirely without pretensions, he was quite clearly and quite rarely, a man happy in his skin.

And as it turned out - a man with a big story.

There are initials for everything nowadays. PTSD is the latest to hit my particular fan. Post Traumatic Stress Disorder - words I've often heard but have not clearly understood. I do now . . . although my words would be Shell Shock. I understand that. I don't want to dwell on the boys in and returning from Iraq and Afghanistan, with this condition.

'Sometimes,' a high up in the Falklands War told me, 'men have had to come home and the great majority respond to treatment. Mostly they return to work.' ('To have another go at getting killed,' I said bitterly.) PTSD in 'normal' circumstances is far less, or not at all, worthy of comment. In any event it's a particularly foul condition, one which Kevin Turner knows only too well.

By the second meeting I was more comfortable with this young man, whom circumstances, Solicitors, Insurance Companies, the accident and well, life really, had thrust upon me out of the blue. Let's face it, he probably didn't particularly want to be there anyway. Why would being courteous and kind to a crabby old woman, especially one with opinions, be his cup of tea? However, courtesy and kindness sit comfortably with Kevin Turner.

As he worked on my back and shoulders and between yelps of pain, mine, we talked. He explained how he was setting about the imposed whiplash, muttering 'stiff as a board' and other uncomplimentary comments as he worked. It all hurt, but it wasn't exactly the Blitz.

Finally, he flopped back into a chair and made more notes. He recognised the symptoms of stress as we talked. He asked about the troubled nights, the anxieties and the tears . . . dragging all the silly unexplained incidents out of me.

He winced as I mentioned the dislocation of the left hip and smiled indulgently when I said I would rather have a multiple birth than go through that again.

'Everything you are saying makes complete sense,' he said. (Oh, good egg,) 'and your reactions are entirely normal.'

Kevin had become not simply Physio, but Counsellor as well.

He actually appeared to understand, to recognise exactly what I was talking about. 'Have you ever dislocated anything?' I asked, 'Because it's not what anyone wants to be doing.' 'Well, yes I have', he replied. 'Ten years ago I

180

broke my neck.'

Hmmmm. What CAN I say? There's really no answer to that. I mean, you can't break your neck . . . and live . . . can you . . . or can you?

In my book, that's a miracle.

Not normally known for being short of a word . . . I was. On this occasion I was fresh out of words. I have to say that in that moment, Kevin had rather put things into perspective. Perhaps by coincidence, perhaps by design. We shall probably never know.

But it was damned clever.

And as the questions came flooding in, he was packing his sort of modern Doctor's bag . . . preparing to leave. Slinging it nonchalantly over his shoulder, (I wonder now, which shoulder,) he was on the drive.

'See you next week,' he said.

And he was gone.

> 'They have their exits and their entrances . . .'
> And that was some exit.

* * *

Getting to the nub of it . . . or at least trying to.

Throughout the following week, I chewed away at this information. Writers are inveterate delvers, obsessive seekers after the truth, always needing to pick at the very bones of the minutiae of the given facts. In this particular case there was nothing I could do, but wait. And marvel . . . and doubt. Ah. But I had glimpsed the scar.

It was true all right, Kevin was alive and well and living in Dorset. As he worked he began to tell me a bit about the day that changed his life. 'It happened,' he said, 'because I had a bike accident. No, a motor bike. I was racing in Holland, Motorbike and Sidecar, and when I crashed, my own bike went over my neck. You must try and persevere with the exercises I have given you or we shall never get this sorted . . . and yes, I do know it hurts . . . The bike always follows the rider, you see. Strange that isn't it?"

He went on making dough on my right shoulder - I went on grumbling - and finally, mercifully he stopped. Sipping black coffee, while I nursed my wounds, he went on, "There was a shemozzle, which I knew very little about, and I landed up in a hospital outside London, near to Reading" . . . (The

181

Middlesex.)

At this point I could only think of his people . . . his parents, his mother, especially. How on earth could she possibly cope seeing him broken like this? And his wife or girlfriend . . . What do you do? How do you react, how do you respond - when something you might well have been dreading, actually happens?

I thought of my own kids who, mercifully, had not been bitten by this particular deadly bug. There were, and had been, plenty of life threatening bugs. I thanked God then and now, that motorbikes had not been one of them.

I sat back, holding my shoulder, rocking slightly. I have no idea if Kevin picked up some disquiet on my part, he's pretty perceptive - people who have been through the mill, usually are.

Anyway, 'That's enough for today,' he said cheerfully and off he went.

It transpired that there was little option to the path his life would take. Motorbikes were to be his destiny . . . and neither did he seek any other. It was in the blood. Kevin came from an extended line of Champions, 3 generations, going right back to his Grandfather. Team Turner were winners - and the grandfather was to figure closely in this story.

So we have this youngster, going through school and probably hating it. 'Why do I have to do all this? I only want to ride, like Dad and Granddad - and I know I'll be good at it, if only you'd all just let me get on with it. I've got all this homework. I don't know what it means, any of it. I can't do it and I don't want to.'

He was rubbing a speck of dust from the tank on his father's bike, using the sleeve of his blazer. 'You see, I could start by keeping all these bikes clean.' There wasn't a mark on any of them. His mother had heard it all before, many times. She put an arm round his shoulder and guided him gently towards the house. 'Come on, let's look at it together,' she said calmly. 'Maybe you weren't listening very well. It will probably all come back when you read it through again. You go up and change and I'll make you a sandwich. But Kevin, if you really don't work at school, at all, then you won't even be able to read properly. You'd have to rely on others reading even the Events calendar to you. You wouldn't like that now, would you?' The boy shuffled off and the mother thought she just might have won that one. 'He'll get there,' she said and she smiled happily.

'. . . and then the schoolboy, with his satchel and shining morning face, creeping like snail, unwillingly to school . . .'

Dreams and Nightmares

Kevin grew of course, into his skin and into his dreams. He was to carry high the flag of Team Turner. Popular, beer swigging - one of the boys. Rugby and Bikes . . . what else is there to do? Except for one thing. Kevin had been blessed with a brain . . . and also with the gift of deductive reasoning, a gift to be tried and tested more than he could ever possibly have foreseen.

He made his people proud, especially his Grandfather - and he loved what he did. The Glory Days.

I don't actually believe the - 'all good things must come to an end' adage. Otherwise whatever is there to strive for? I do however, believe the others . . . 'when one door closes, another opens' and also 'An opportunity is what you get, when you don't get what you want.' So we shall see.

Fast forward to the terrible accident, to this young fit man, lying in a hospital bed, with his neck broken. After receiving the best treatment available to him at the time, he was given the unbelievable news that he and his family were dreading and which the hospital hated to deliver. He was told that they had done all they could for him and it was with great regret they also had to tell him that he must face the fact that in six months he would be confined to a wheelchair. He was 27 years old. A young man with his life before him. There was no further treatment.

I cannot begin to imagine how he, how all of them, must have felt. The evening he arrived home, however, the phone rang and a voice asked to speak to him. He took the phone and a European voice said, 'Kevin, I can help . . .' He, Kevin, replaced the phone immediately, believing it was one of his friends, fooling around. A somewhat sick joke. After a few moments the phone rang again and the same voice said, 'Kevin, don't hang up, please. I believe I can help you.'
Oh my God. And I mean just that.

* * *

Enter Phenomenal Miracle Medic

It transpired that the voice belonged to a Dutch Orthopaedic Surgeon who was a motor bike race enthusiast. He had actually been on site, watching the race and had witnessed these momentous events. He had also, apparently, kept an eye on Kevin's ensuing progress throughout. He was, I think, one of only two Surgeons in the world, at that time, who was able to perform the required operation which would save Kevin's life - and hopefully enable him to walk again.

The Turner family crowded round the phone and then, understandably, burst into action A few days later Kevin was on the table in theatre in the hospital, in Holland, not far from the spot where the accident had occurred. It is possible that the same operation is performed now, routinely.

At that time it was ground breaking.

Kevin survived . . . Is there anyone out there who doesn't believe in miracles? Please read on.

'And then the young man - full of strange oaths and bearded like the Pard . . .'

CONCENTRATE

Concentrate Jane. We'll do just one more exercise and then you can stop. Head and neck. Oh no. Not head and neck. That hurts so much. Come on, it will hurt less and less the more you do it . . . especially if you would practice every day. I can't. Actually, I just can't. And anyway you are a sadist. You can go off people, you know. Yeah right!

Now, nice straight back. Head to the left. Further, you can do better than that. Two, Three . . . That'll do won't it. I'll do more when you've gone. And anyway, what am I, an owl? Four, Five, Six. Hmm. You haven't done much work on that, have you? Sorry, I've had so much to do . . . Anyway, you wouldn't like it. I bet you wouldn't do it. Jane, I've done more of all this stuff than you've had hot dinners. Head to the right. Two, Three, Four. Can I stop now? Both sides again? You haffta be joking . . . Oh, all RIGHT. O K. That'll do. You can stop now. But do try to work on these exercises. It will get easier . . . Praise Be.

Kevin dropped easily into a chair and started his notes. I staggered painfully over to make the coffee.

'What on earth ever made you become a Physio,' I asked. 'I can't think of anything worse.

'It was a bit odd I suppose,' he said. 'A lady suggested it'. I had a vision of this Wilkie Collins character, dressed in floaty grey gossamer, drifting in and out of view. Mind you, I was tired at the time . . . I pulled myself together.

'This lady,' I said. 'Was she actually there? Alive, I mean. A person, a sentient being. Or maybe a ghost?'

'She was my Physio', he said. And off he went.

Silly me. Amazing what fatigue can do.

I quizzed him again at the next session. Why can't I just let sleeping dogs lie. And it came to pass that that lady had sown the seed of Kevin's future. And of course she was right. He was an obvious candidate with exactly the right personality. He had done it all and seen it all.

Someone else in the right place at the right time. Odd, n'est ce pas?

Kevin Turner walks in the light.

I asked Kevin once if he realised how blessed he is . . . does he have a belief in God, in a Deity, in Angels. 'Well, not re - e - ally,' he replied, 'although

185

I do know there is something . . . I did ask my Grandfather, before every race, to look after me.' He clutched his lapel as he spoke . . . He believed that. Well there you are. That's good enough for me.

Kevin has a Guardian Angel.

Kevin Turner went back to school. To University that is. Three years, four years . . . and retrained. BUT . . . and this is what this piece is all about. . . . After he had qualified he got back on the bike. Oh no. I covered my face. I wished I hadn't asked. 'Had to,' he said. 'It meant I had to train again . . . to get fit . . . to work out. And I was looking for closure . . . I knew it would give me closure. I arranged to do three more races, and that would be it.'

And that was it . . . Deductive Reasoning.

'An opportunity to grow is what you get when you don't get what you want'

Kevin will go forth now, sharing his light, for that is his destiny.

* * *

The Physio's Nightmare . . . The Realist

The joints that I have - are all that I have,
And the joints that I have are mine . . .
And the pain that I have,
In the joints that I have,
Is mine. . . and mine . . . and mine.
A hope I shall have,
An Op I shall have,
Relief will be for a time . . .
But the pain in my joints,
In the long, long years,
Will be mine - and mine - and mine!

Sorry Kev.

Dave

Part X

Dogs - Dogs - Dogs

Pooh Bear

Three cheers for Pooh
For who?
For Pooh.
Why what did he do?
Oh, I thought you knew
he saved his friend from a wetting.

Three cheers for Bear!
For where?
For Bear,
he couldn't swim
but he rescued him.
Rescued who?
Oh, listen do,
I'm speaking of Pooh.
Of who?
Of Pooh.
Oh, you don't care . . .
Of Bear!

From Winnie the Pooh. A. A. Milne.

BEAR - A Yorkshire Terrier

Of course, then there was Bear. It can't be all good. Bear was one of those entirely unseen, unprovoked and indescribably ghastly events that happen in families from time to time.

He was a three pound, eighteen inch, uncontainable bundle of every thing you never want to confront and certainly never want to give space. It all happened so easily, so simply and so entirely unexpectedly.

Amanda I and were jogging along, running the shop, Long Hall Antiques, in Wareham, Dorset. I don't know that we knew very much about anything, but we learned very quickly. We had taken over a big old house which had been a Doctor's Surgery. The room which had been the Waiting Room had a fairly big bay window, an obvious Shop. Contained within this space we installed a staircase, which led to a room of equal size. Amanda took herself, together with her stock, up there and I held court in the ground floor room. It was great fun. My stock was posh junk really, which was what I knew a lot about and Amanda had a sort of Aladdin's Cave of ephemera (which I see in Chamber's is 'a fly that lives for one day only' and that is not at all what I mean.) What I  mean is that Amanda's stock was different - a treasure trove of interesting and exciting artefacts from all over the world. The Dealers put us on their buying route and mostly derided my stock and shuffled fairly quickly upstairs. Of course, she was young and pretty and long discussions ensued, usually over prolonged cups of coffee. Questions of condition, provenance, age, value, and saleability seemed to go on endlessly but there is no doubt that when her items sold, the

 Dealers went off well pleased and left Amanda able to buy the food that week. But I expect I was good at something. And it was just about then that Amanda fell in love. Not with a nice eligible young man from the environs, nor with one of our endless stream of dealers from across the world, (although there were a few of those, of course). No, that would have been far too normal. And by now, if you haven't already lost the will to live, you may think that all this has very little to do with Bear. And there you would be very wrong, beggin' your pardon, for it was with Bear she fell in love, hook, line and sinker.

Bear was a Yorkshire Terrier with a long pedigree and black and tan hair to match. Amanda occupied the rooms at the top of the house, which we made into a large flat. That was her first line of attack.

'Would it be all right if I had a very small dog?' she asked innocently, one day. We already had Golda, a yellow Labrador, and a fiendish black and white cat called Pig. So of course, in what seemed to me to be an entirely reasonable response, I just said, 'Well not really, darling, it wouldn't work, would it?' I lost that battle, like so many others, and Bear duly took up residence. 'You need never see him actually,' she said. 'I will keep him in a box upstairs; I will walk him, groom him and feed him. And Golda will love him.' Yeah, right!

She did feed him, sometimes, mostly on cat food (bought by me). She had him groomed at vast expense, by a lady who lived 25 miles away, and from whom he returned, glossy coat sweeping the floor, looking uncommonly proud. How like a man. And to be fair, she did take him for daily exercise. To the Pub.

A few yards along the road from us, on the other side, was The King's Arms . . . and routinely this pair, she tall, elegant and 20 something and he, 6 months or so and hairy, set out on their daily mission to walk the dog. First the road had to be negotiated and Bear learned very smartly to 'stop and sit' at the crossing. He knew the sound of the 'cross now' pips and getting up decorously, head held high, tail ditto, he took his mistress safely across, straight into the pub and into the company of his appreciative and vocal audience.

This was the dog walk, which took place on a daily basis. Well, he was only a little dog and he did have to walk there AND back.

More about Bear

For a dog already labelled a waste of space I must say he's getting a very good innings. This piece was all about Amanda really and Bear played such a big part.

For a while life went on in Long Hall and it included Bear. The first thing he did was to sidle up to Golda like a long lost product of the long spayed womb. He stepped gently into her basket, intending to cuddle up, (he had only just left a litter of siblings) but Golda wasn't having any of it and as Bear stepped in, she stepped gently out. That pattern continued for all time. We all have our limits.

The cat was a different scenario.

From day one the Pig and the Bear loathed each other with a great loathing.

Cat was truly displaced and I never remember him jumping down onto the kitchen floor again when Bear was there. It was more of a protest really. He had always come and gone through the kitchen window and now he made that area his own. The sill was wide and upon this was placed a red chenille cushion, gold banded, a bowl of fresh milk and at regular intervals a dish of expensive food.

Cat came to the very edge of a cupboard and there he sat, sweeping his luxurious tail just out of reach, uttering unrepeatable feline expletives. This display of barely disguised aggression worked Dog into a frenzy of reciprocal animus. And so we lived. And so much for 'I'll keep him in a box in my room, Mummy.'

That was when I learned to question more or less everything anyone said to me ever again.

One day, Amanda announced that she was going to London to take up an offer from an Antique Dealer she knew, who was going to employ her while teaching her art appreciation, and she would be taking Bear. Praise Be.

Life quickly reverted to normal. Cat took his meals once again from the dish on the kitchen floor, sauntered into the sitting room and curled up happily by the fire, or lay purring on the chesterfield, no doubt dreaming smug dreams of splendid victories in the canine arena. But it didn't last.

Apparently, Ted Few, wife, family and friends couldn't stand it either. They had an ancient Old English Sheepdog called Gyp. Amanda's room was on the second floor of their house and was approached by a loft ladder. No doubt you can guess what is coming . . . Bear spent his nights prancing round the open aperture screaming at Gyp, who lay below in a curly rolled up heap muttering soft complacent sighs, as befits one of advanced years. Bear had to go.

Of course I protested loudly, banged the table, stamped the foot and just said NO, to pleadings and bribes and tears . . . 'would you just have him for three weeks . . . Please Mum, PLEEEESE, just while I get a flat . . .'

I lost that one too and the three weeks turned into fourteen years.

Like all, most, Yorkies, Bear made up for his lack of height with 'poisonality plus.' He had the heart and courage of a lion and was entirely fearless. He was extremely territorial and quickly established the pecking order. This is my patch . . . keep off. He chased away all birds, whatever their size, but cats remained his very special bête noire and you wouldn't give much for any who chanced their tails and entered hallowed ground.

Gone the long sweeping straight coat, I snipped that off very quickly, he always enjoyed a bath and suffered necessary frequent brushing. He went on journeys of exploration all the time, he had altercations constantly with chicken, sheep, cattle and their irate owners, he terrorised everyone and everything in sight. He had become a country dog.

And how I loved him.

Haughty friend Max   Bear and Lady

For Lady

A black Labrador – 2nd June 1997

Tears in the swirling noises in my ears . . .

Tears in the stinging dryness in my eyes . . .

Tears in the wooden numbness of my cheek . . .

Tears in the aching thickness of my throat . . .

Tears in the stumbling quiet of my voice . . .

Tears in the choking catches of my breath . . .

Tears in the careless pumping of my heart . . .

Tears in the gaping empty of my soul . . .

Tears for the love of a lady . . .

Who quiet, died today.

Part XI

Tooting Bec Gardens

Three Fair Princesses

We do not often meet.
And when we meet we cannot speak . . . or understand.
But you have found the universal language -
The Language of the SMILE.
That smile in passing, will always open doors.
I hope you will remember your holiday with fondness and giggles.
You will remember coming into this big old house - full of big old
furniture and strange pictures gazing down from the walls.
Other people's pictures and artefacts say so much about their owner.
You will remember Amanda.
A whirlwind in the morning
Full of toast and love and joy - But I will tell you a secret.
At 7pm she turns into a DORMOUSE. What about that.
And Lily is quite the opposite - she hates the hours before 11am
and wants to sleep.
In the evening, however - she becomes a party-girl.
This is all very confusing. But she is very kind. And funny. And Smiley.
You will remember New Year's Eve - in London in 2008.
You will perhaps remember the shadowy old lady who exchanged big smiles -
when she creaked along to the bathroom . . .
And she will remember you.
Three happy girls who say a thousand words
in the eloquence of their smiles.

Oma Jane XXX

30th December 2008

The Elf and the Dormouse

Under a toadstool crept a wee Elf,
Out of the rain to shelter herself.

Under a toadstool fast asleep.
Sat a big Dormouse all in a heap.

Trembled the wee Elf, frightened and yet
Fearing to fly away, lest she got wet.

To the next shelter, maybe a mile,
Sudden the wee Elf smiled a wee smile.

Tugged til the toadstool toppled in two,
Holding it over her, gaily she flew.

Soon she was safe home, dry as could be.
Soon woke the Dormouse . . .'Good gracious me!

Where is my toadstool?' Loud he lamented
And that's how umbrellas first were invented.

QUACK! QUACK!

Oliver Herford.

Just one of those days . . .

Gremlins all around . . .
cutting the finger . . .
spilling the water . . .
spoiling the floor . . .
Meece in the cupboard . . .
Can't bear no more.

Fairies move in . . .
Wings iridescent . . .
Hair fair and flying . . .
Little wands sparkling.

I'd trod on me glasses . . .
It isn't a joke . . .
Flash of the wand . . .
Glasses ain't broke.

Blew love on the finger . . .
Mopped up the floor . . .
Like the Pied Piper . . .
Peeped in at the door.

Laughing and tinkling . . .
Away in a trice . . .
Riding astride on . . .
The backs of the mice.

All better . . . smiley face.

Jane

February 2012.

Every Cloud . . . For Lily

Hey Belle . . . Look up at that big black cloud,
heavy and floppy,
like the face of a child with a puckered smile,
scooting across the dense grey sky.

Hey! Look up at the cloud again . . .
See the frilly silver edge,
chasing its cloud, dancing and shining?
Scooting across the dense grey sky.

Plop, plop, here comes the rain . . .
Open your hands . . . magic pearls drop on to your palms,
and hey! Look up, the cloud is still there . . .
scooting across the dense grey sky.

Oh and now, here comes the sun, bossy and yellow.
And watch: the cloud is changing. It is shining too!
All turned silver, like a silver frill.
That is called its Lining. Every cloud has one.

Every cloud has a silver lining. And so will this one.
And hey Belle. You can always make it happen.

Love,

As a matter of fact this piece should probably be renamed, 'UCAS Mayhem'!

So Belle darling, there we are . . . I actually wrote it some time ago. I
expect something else was happening. It passed, as will this. I didn't send it.
Perhaps I thought you were too young. Now perhaps you are too old.

However, it was written for you and you might like to have it.

You know I love you, always and forever.

Go for it, Belle.

For Lily . . . A Levels 2010

If

If you can keep your head when all about you
Are losing theirs and blaming it on you;
If you can trust yourself when all men doubt you,
But make allowance for their doubting too:
If you can wait and not be tired by waiting,
Or, being lied about, don't deal in lies,
Or being hated don't give way to hating,
And yet don't look too good, nor talk too wise;

If you can dream - and not make dreams your master;
If you can think - and not make thoughts your aim,
If you can meet with Triumph and Disaster
And treat those two impostors just the same:
If you can bear to hear the truth you've spoken
Twisted by knaves to make a trap for fools,
Or watch the things you gave your life to, broken,
And stoop and build 'em up with worn-out tools;

If you can make one heap of all your winnings
And risk it on one turn of pitch-and-toss,
And lose, and start again at your beginnings,
And never breathe a word about your loss:
If you can force your heart and nerve and sinew
To serve your turn long after they are gone,
And so hold on when there is nothing in you
Except the Will which says to them: 'Hold on!'

If you can talk with crowds and keep your virtue,
Or walk with Kings - nor lose the common touch,
If neither foes nor loving friends can hurt you,
If all men count with you, but none too much:
If you can fill the unforgiving minute
With sixty seconds' worth of distance run,
Yours is the Earth and everything that's in it,
And - which is more - you'll be a Man, my son!

Rudyard Kipling 1895

IGNATIOUS LOYOLA . . .

Mystic - Educator - Preacher and Founder of The Jesuits. 1491 - 1556

Teach us, good Lord to serve thee as thou deservest,

to give and not to count the cost;

to fight and not to heed the wounds;

to toil and not to seek for rest;

to labour and not to ask for any reward;

except that of knowing that we do thy will. Amen

The Counsel of Perfection

And if you can do any or all of that - You'll be a Saint, my son.

We can but try!

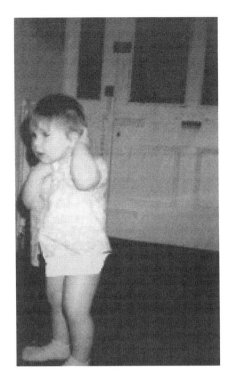
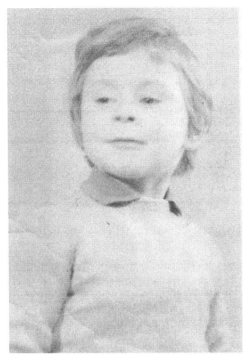

Coming Home . . .

Turning into the long gravelly drive,
tiny pears forming on retreating blossom,
Marguerites and Alstroemeria already high,
weeds also strong and healthy . . .
arriving at the tall iron gates,
and peering through the bars . . .
it lay before me, spread and painted
like a Monet.
Home.

Oh, but I do miss you, my girls.
The very essence of regenerated life.
Through pillars into peaceful Edwardiana . . .
Away from the London streets,
Too many cars . . .
Into the hubble bubble of children and homework,
Too many words.
Through sunshine doors into the whispering of the Willow
and the clamour of birdsong in Spring.
Too many notes.
Home.

But here in this Dorset garden,
trees everywhere, in near full leaf,
even the Ash, recovering from recent surgery,
shakes leafy fingers to welcome back the Jackdaws.
All except the Mulberry - who with her three hundred years -
creaks slowly through her knotted joints,
to spread the ultimate canopy.

The Spinney, a haze of nodding bluebells,
the walls a shroud of pendulous Wisteria,
and in the rose garden, forbidden Drive
and hidden crevices . . . Forget me nots . . .
Like it or not, they will have their place.

On the lower lawn, hugely pregnant peonies,
unashamedly ready to burst, rub shoulders with hydrangeas,
in similar condition.

On the Rose arch, a delicate Clematis, mingles happily,
in peaceful coexistence, awaiting the Honeysuckle.
And the militant Phormium - reaching, straining,
this year it means to touch the clouds.
Too many plants?

But you should see the Choysia -
Up on the top lawn, near to the temple
staring into the dawn,
a vast white starburst, smiling.

There is no doubt, this is Home . . .
But oh! I do miss you,
My girls.
My loved ones.

Part XII

Discovering Creswell Hall

We had been searching for a long time. Wanting to get further West. Nothing seemed quite right. Nothing quite worth the move. After all, the house we had was lovely. Perhaps it had simply served its turn. Perhaps we just had itchy feet.

We had lived in Wareham, in Dorset, for some years. Long Hall came out of the blue really. An old stone house, on the little High Street, sitting comfortably next to the Post Office. Like most of the properties there, it was several hundred years old and seemed perfectly happy to welcome us, as it had dozens of families before us - and to share with us its long history.

We discovered from the Agent's particulars that it had been the Doctor's Surgery, so it was fairly big. There was masses to do, within the bounds of Listed requirements. There were ancient features everywhere, which we would not have dreamed of altering. We set about the work with great gusto and quickly (?) knocked it into shape. Ah! To be young.

We ended up with a lovely old house, on three floors - all the space we could have asked for and a delightful garden . . . but what to do? How usefully, to spend the time? Well, open an Antique shop, of course. And that is exactly what we did. It wasn't a particularly easy ride. There were permissions and all sorts of legal stuff we knew nothing about, to overcome. But we didn't know much about failure either, then. And we had such a lot of help, from so many people . . . people who did know. Long Hall Antiques was born.

It was the greatest fun. We made mistakes, we bought, sometimes unwisely, with the heart, that is - almost always an unwise move - and we pulled off the occasional coup. It is the occasional coup, which thankfully, saved our bacon and allowed us to buy again. 'You buy, or you die'

Amanda bravely started trading in France. They liked her and her pretty Franglais. And she loved them and still does, she did well and quickly learned exactly what she was good at and concentrated upon those specific areas. She still has that particular 'eye', now splendidly refined and extended. But I digress.

For a piece entitled, 'Discovering Creswell Hall,' that preamble is long. Fun though.

Ages later, just when we were despairing of ever finding another nest, it happened. The Postman, on his rounds one day, stopped at our door . . . and a large foolscap envelope plopped on to the rug. Without picking it up I looked at it and weighed up the pros and cons. Too big to be from the Bank . . . too small to be say, a Summons . . . wrong colour for mindless rubbish . . . So what on earth was it? Oh, the pain.

But I needn't have worried. For once it was nothing sinister or menacing. It was a missive from the Estate Agent - nothing scary there, probably just useless. 'The mixture as before'.

But as I pulled the papers from the big envelope it began to look as if it could be a bit interesting and in full view it looked not only interesting . . . it looked wonderful.

The photograph showed a fairly large, gabled, Hamstone house with leaded lights and a couple of long bays with French doors. There was an additional section thrown on at one end, which looked earlier than the rest. An old Welsh slate roof covered the whole and that looked in a reasonable state.

But it was a photograph, an Estate Agent's photograph at that, which attracted me. I sat down on the bottom stair, the better to digest and dissect the information, looking first at the price. It was just about do-able. But the house did seem big . . . Too big. Nothing daunted, I took the whole thing up to Amanda, still lounging in bed . . . 9.30am. But not for long. She was as intrigued as I and together we pored over the information, passing and re-passing the sheets of words and photographs between us.

First, location. It was still Dorset, about fifty miles to the west, straight along the coast. An hour away. Perfect. A quick phone call to the Agent and we were on our way. Creswell, here we come.

The road from Wareham to Creswell is spectacularly beautiful, running as it does east to west along the Jurassic Coast. Quite literally, over the hills and far away. Through small villages nestling into the hills, through farmland, fields of crops lovingly tended and cattle and sheep grazing on land where generations of animals had grazed before. Houses and cottages dotted around in the lee of the slopes and through the valleys - and the prize, the sea, sometimes just a tantalizing glimpse, sometimes a wide promise. Surely, no one can ever be unmindful, unseeing, of this constancy of time and beauty. However often I take this road, it never fails to impress me with joy.

So Creswell, a village often passed through en route to Exeter, had every chance of being a winner and so of course did the house on offer, with no pressure or persuasion from the Agent. But never tell him that. We were dealers and there might be a deal to be done.

Meeting that worthy at the appointed place, we followed him. At the church he turned left. So did we. We had entered a small lane, and passing a row of pretty cottages, we quickly turned left again. Then after a hundred yards or so we all turned left again, into a long gravel drive. Pear trees and roses rambled all along a stone wall and we passed an old building on the left.

We seem to have gone full circle.

At the top of the drive, there it lay, just as the photo had portrayed. We stood for a moment, breathing it in - and finally we understood. We had indeed gone full circle - in time as well as in perception.

As we had travelled along the village road, we had passed the Georgian front, (or had it been the back?). But wait, this must surely be the front, (or was it the back?). No doubt the Agent had marked this reaction before and he smiled whimsically. 'Shall we go in?' he said.

He turned a huge key in the lock of a heavily studded, vastly thick oak door and we passed into a lobby and then into the hall . . . but actually, not the hall - a 'front hall'. The hall proper was further in, through an arched entrance. It was rather grand, housing a fireplace in a stone surround and a quite spectacular oak staircase. There was a typical Georgian sash window with wooden glazing bars and the normal window seat. 'Ah, I see,' Amanda and I chorused together. 'We have come full circle. That is the road.' And so it was. The house stood firmly on the road. . . . Ah. Was this to be the first Deal Breaker? We listened . . . Not a sound. These walls were two or three hundred years old and a bit of Twentieth Century traffic was not going to cause any problem here.

Agent's particulars are almost always adequate, taken from the best angle to show this or that to the very best advantage, to give an impression of space - but invariably they lack something. They lack the essence, the soul, the spirit of the place. This house had all those things and I so wondered why . . . what else was it I could feel?

Love. It was, of course, love.

We followed the Agent into the Drawing Room; finely proportioned and gloriously symmetrical, which suited my O.C.D very well, a high ceiling with two huge oak beams running the full width . . . and a central broad Minster Stone open fireplace, sporting an embossed Family Crest.

There were two large, tall, leaded windows, each with a window seat, one south facing, and the other looking east. There was also a French door. The wall into which these were all set was at least two feet thick. The weather was an Estate Agent's dream and the sun came flooding in, filling the entire room with golden light. 'Shall we sit down for a moment?' said he. 'Let me tell you a bit about the house, you seem to like what you have viewed so far.' We said nothing . . . We were not getting caught by that one. 'As you have perceived, the house is of two distinct periods . . . the roadside on the north is Georgian while this side, the south face, is far younger, almost contemporary.' He was a bit precious, but none the worse for all that and I'm afraid we did not produce the obligatory gasp.

We had sort of worked that out for ourselves and were trying desperately not to jump about in sheer delight . . . We were in love.

'This house,' he went on, warming to his task . . . (we so wanted to get on with the tour and sweep up the wonderful staircase, but we sat, hands folded demurely in laps like expectant fifth formers and listened - to what I have to say was an intriguing story.)

'This house was the vision of a retired Judge. A man who loved the area with a passion. Together with his wife, he had visited many times to get away from the hurly-burly of London, and whenever they were down they looked around, thinking of the day they could move - lock, stock and barrel and fulfil their dream.'

Chauffeur driven, in a beautiful Rolls Royce, they travelled at a steady speed, seldom at more than twenty miles per hour and they traversed the County of Dorset. Time and time again they came, never hurried, always hopeful, that each time they would find it, that they would discover their jewel - as of course they did. Rather like us, some seventy or eighty years later, they found the village of Creswell. The year was, I think, about 1915 and they had found their house.

They purchased it, together with a large parcel of land, bounded to the east by the river. On the west there started the row of cottages, still there today and to the south a little country lane, which still meanders down to the sea.

'Of course,' the Agent was saying. 'It was a tremendous project the Judge was undertaking and one which he tackled with great gusto. Carefully chosen Architects and Designers were selected. Builders, plumbers and decorators were brought in and slowly and steadily the work proceeded. But it was the Judge who had vision. It was he who brought the passion, the love. Nothing was side tracked, nothing was neglected. Only the best was good enough. In its time it was perfection.'

He stopped for breath and reviewed his, now really attentive, audience. He had us eating out of his hand. He stood up and led us out of the room and back into the main hall. He pointed out the archway joining the two halls. 'Look at the depth of this wall,' he said. 'This is the original back wall of the two cottages which form the front . . . back . . . north of the house. It runs straight - east to west - and contains within it all the chimneys. It is to this wall that the Judge and his army of workers literally joined the back . . . front . . . south face as you see it today.

You will agree I am sure, that it was quite inspired.' Oh yes. We agreed, wholeheartedly. As we walked around, up and down, it was all entirely clear and all entirely beautiful.

At last we climbed the wonderful staircase.

Wide, shallow treads carried us gently up. The generous banister rail, with turned and rounded spindles, glowed with a much lovingly polished patina and on each newel post dwelt a commemorative carving.

The wide landing just followed the wall and bathrooms and workrooms came off to the north, while the south, the new addition, housed the spacious and light bedrooms, more or less a mirror image of the ground floor. Recalling it now, it all sounds so easy, so obvious. But think of the time, the sheer hard graft and the love that went into it.

Especially the love.

* * *

Eventually we were on our way home. We were completely exhausted. Too tired even to talk, we just drove - back along the coast - over the hills and far away - back through the beauty - in the setting sun.

And the next day the sale of our house in Wareham fell through. Panic stations. Then we knew, we really knew, how much we wanted that house, how right it was.

It worked out, mercifully, as things do, if they are meant to be. And all that was in 1987. Thirty years ago. How can that be? I know I have spoken a lot about the love that I felt dwelt in this house. It was true then. It is true today.

Love has to be reciprocal if it is to be of value - and that is how it has been. I have cherished the house and the house has been kind to me, unbelievably so. Of course it hasn't all been easy. Nothing ever is, but with the co-operation of the Judge and house, it has been manageable.

There has been asset stripping, never easy, never desirable . . . but given the choice, if it meant I could stay . . . no contest. The first major outlay was the north roof - in fact the entire roof - had to be rebuilt . . . A cottage was sold.

215

When life became untenable with the turbulent Priest, he had to go and so did the tennis court.

Perhaps the saddest thing on the survival trail, once I was alone, was facing up to selling the west wing - to actually diminish the house. Or leave.

With a heavy heart plans were drawn. When it came to it, it was not so utterly devastating as I had envisaged . . . w - e - e - l - l.

Remember, the front - back, the original house, had been two Georgian cottages on the road. So in point of fact they merely had to be divided off again . . . Simple.

But I shall never forget that wall. The dividing wall - massive, huge, Berlin, are all words which spring readily to mind, even now. And foundations which went down to the bowels of the earth. So no, it was not, of course, simple - far from it, but with endless discussion with a very patient Architect, a lot of tweaking, some dog-legging and a great deal of prayer and tears, the division was achieved.

Oh, Woe.

But hearken, oh ye of little faith - for there is always Hope. The wall covers and encompasses three connecting doors - one on each floor. Open them up, three vast oak lintels and hey presto, the house magically becomes one again. And somewhere, at some time, someone may be guided by the Judge, to do just that.

Oh Joy.

A strip of garden, to give access, had to be included and so did the biggest and best shed in the world. Oh no. That means a fence and I really hate naked fences. But of course, it could quickly be covered with shrubs, rambler roses anything. And everything.

The day came when a prospective purchaser arrived. Poor man. I am sure I was particularly foul to him and he certainly did not deserve that. However he neither knew nor cared - even if he noticed - and the deal was done.

He moved in and we have been friends ever since. Not only friends but really good neighbours - he is as anti social as I.

But we care about each other, he watches to see I am the right way up and occasionally we have a very large brandy together.

But additionally, he loves the house too and so does his family. So we get along very well.

CHANT . . . in full Regalia (Choir Boy)

And the man said unto me -
Tread not upon this ground -
For the place whereon ye stand -
Is hallowed land.

And furthermore, quoth he -
Approach not ye this shed -
For in so doing, listen well -
Many men have bled.

The land around is mined -
I say this only once -
That there within this simple shed -
A dart, so small, but evil yet -
Is trained upon thine head.

BE WARNED THIS DAY . . .
The First Day in the Ninth Month In the Two thousand and
Twelfth moon -
In the year of Our Fear'ed Leader.

For Colin – 'im next door

And we still had the Chapel - the early bit, the original bit that dwells quietly to the east.

That was the house . . . so now to set about the garden.

And that was a mammoth task, rather tear stained at first. All these walls and fences and things, intruding all over the place. The wall which divides off the new house on the tennis court is rather amazing, if you like that sort of thing. All the stone, natural Hamstone, was cut to size on site and topped with flat half pavers. So it is quite a work of art - but it had to be hidden - with trees, of course. Brought up in the New Forest and with a passion for trees, I quickly bought them.

Twin eight foot container grown Weeping Willows came home with me in the car, and now, twenty something years later, they are more than twenty something feet high and their swaying branches gently sweep the lawns beneath. Then I found a little nut tree in the spinney and also the smallest sycamore, in a crevice where it had gently flown on its propeller - and taken root. I know they are considered 'thugs' and best avoided, but I was on a camouflage mission - in it went, with all the others, together with anything else I could beg or steal.

Now hear this - the beautiful wall is at last, suitably clad. Well I like it anyway. Strangely, there are those who do not.

Wall, what wall?

Up on the top lawn I put in a mighty Oak in memory of the New Forest - not a particularly clever move since it will take many years to become recognisable, but it has put down strong roots and is there for the duration. Fighting for space and light up there is also a Scots Pine, already with beautiful blue fronds.

In the frenzy for forest I made mistakes. Four in all and they are called Cypresses. 'Instant cover - fast growing', says the catalogue. And that is true. Too late, you realise it says nothing about density, black out curtains or non see through fabric - nor that those pretty little Christmas trees grow into something fairly hideous, which you don't have the heart to remove because you love trees. But believe me, they really ARE thugs. And another is Spotted Laurel . . . and another, Bay.

We have all, in abundance.

But let us not dwell upon our mistakes, rather let us dwell upon our successes. And a resounding success has been the Terrace.

A terrace of sorts was there from the beginning of our incumbency. Situated beyond the gravel turning circle, on the south side of the south front and raised by about three feet upon a stone wall, was the somewhat tired terrace, unevenly paved. A further wall beyond and around, planted with established, nicely trailing rockery plants, set the approach off very effectively.

But in the midst of the garden, of all that had been before, all the space, in its entirety - the terrace had no particular need to shine. The whole massive area shone - spread like a tapestry, in the glory of the setting sun as it gently retired, golden and constant, over the woods beyond. The terrace had been simply a part of it all - without pretension but with great potential. And we needed to make the very best of that potential . . . Simple.

Dear John, who had long been helping us to pull this remainder of the garden into shape, set about this colossal task, with great energy. John was young then. We were all young then.

First the area needed levelling, from back to front. This involved removing all the stone - and relaying it, evenly and flat. Job done. Oh, um, but sorry John, not quite. There were just a couple of things - well three, really, before you get too far on with it. I was wondering if a pair of rectangular ponds, there and there, symmetrical to the whole, with a central walk way, would look rather good. What do you think?

'I think it sounds like a great deal of work,' he said solemnly. He took off his cap, scratched his head and replaced the cap. He was playing for time and he can't be blamed for that. Suddenly the job had grown.

'It's about time I knocked off for today, anyway' he said. 'Let me think about it, consider the matter, see what's involved. You think about it too, you might get over it.'

He thought - and I didn't, get over it, that is. In fact, by his next visit I was really excited at the prospect - had drawn it out and everything. I have to say that he came, ready to start. He was pacing it out trying not to look excited himself. He got stuck in, there and then. He really is a star. And I kept quiet about the third thing.

Laboriously, the job took shape. Let not anyone ever believe it was 'simple'. It was hard . . . It was really hard.

But the Terrace was achieved, complete with ponds, and is a resounding success. John planted a James Grieve in a little circle of earth, which he enclosed with edging stones. I planted all the stone containers. Seats, figures and objects were placed strategically.

And now . . . Job done, not simple . . . but simply wonderful.

Amanda, a professional Gardener, arrived just at the right time.
I asked what I should put all around, to contain this masterpiece.
'Well, you'd better have a bit of balustrade,' she said . . .
So balustrade we have. Very lovely it looks . . .
And the house approves.

The Terrace, deserving of an upper case T, has attained its potential,
and more.

Stepping back into the house, warm and welcoming, we are all well pleased. Worthy of comment is the fact that Amanda had arrived together with a film crew, or were they her fellow gardeners, during the Digging Deep period? It doesn't really matter because the net result is the same.

There was this crowd of boys, about four or five of them, all huge, hairy and hungry, loud and jolly - full of jokes, conversation, Politics and differing points of view. And noise. The thing they had in common was a general and constant need to eat . . . and drink.

Mercifully, the food seemed to arrive in take-away bags while the beer came from a constant supply in the boot of one of the cars. And then there was the problem of beds. It was a long time since my own student days and as there was no sign of their moving on, I started fussing about beds and linen.

'Oh, don't worry about all that, darling,' said Amanda, 'you have your bed and I have mine, so we're all right. They'll just sleep where they fall, if you're sure you don't mind.' I had little choice. 'You go on up and I shall come and say Good night.' I went on up.

For the next few days the pattern persisted. They went off each morning, dressed appropriately and looking weird, in varying stages of life and death. 'They'll be OK,' said the daughter who had clearly done it all before. 'Get some fresh air inside them and they'll be ready for work.' They had nothing else inside them so I rather doubted that. I watched the wobbly convoy of cars as it made its way uncertainly down the drive. I bided my time. I had hatched a cunning plan - which in the event was not necessary.

On the day before their departure, Amanda said, sipping coffee, as one after another the boys came into the kitchen, looking relatively sober but not particularly jolly, 'This is our last day, (praise be) and you have been so good having us all here, that we propose giving today to you. What pressing job would you like us to do - What would help most?' In that moment I loved them all . . . I didn't even mind the permeating smell of booze. To be honest, I hadn't expected this - I thought I would have to at least wheedle my way, either by stealth or blackmail, into persuading them, but they were offering.

Without a word on my part, my cunning plan was going to be reality. The Third Thing! And quite a horrible job I had for them, which entailed much digging out and heaving of earth, a lot of grunting and drinking - in this case of the soft variety - cheese sandwiches by the mile and fervent promises of shepherd's pie, bangers and mash and BEER . . . Steps were taken and steps were built.

By the end of the day, I had my stone steps, five in all and each four feet wide, from the Terrace up to the top lawn. An enduring victory for the young and such a great gift.

And now, looking back, I so love my house. I have resisted my kids telling me it's about time I moved and found somewhere smaller and more sensible, really just by asking plaintively, 'Where am I supposed to go?' And even the son coughs and says Hmmm. And so I live here, hermitoid and happy - coexisting with those who came before - the unlikely smell of pipe tobacco in the hall, the knowledge of the little serving girl, dressed in early costume, looking on, the occasional chattering in the aura . . . and the love.

Always the love.

Steps were taken and steps were built

And we still have the Chapel . . .

We still have the Chapel, the early bit, the original bit which dwells quietly to the east. The Chapel is a very special bit of the whole. It may be Georgian the same as its adjoining bit . . . but I am not sure. I think it is earlier. It feels earlier. A serene space, breathing tranquillity.

It has always been called The Chapel in my time. And in fact, as I was told by a member of the previous family, it was used as a family chapel during their incumbency and previously. 'Alter and candles,' she said. 'There and there.'

Be that as it may, the Chapel now has a special function.

Years ago, when my brother was living in Scotland (alone, as it turned out, other members of the family having deserted or come South) I had the idea of converting the Chapel into a separate unit for him, despite dire warnings from my sister Rachel, the kindest and mildest of people.

'He won't stay in there you know. He'll come in, sit in your armchair, just when you are settling down, smoke his evil smelling cigarettes and drop ash and fag ends all around his chair on your carpet, burn it and not even notice.'

Oh, Wow. She obviously had experience.

However I persisted and continued, with the builders creating their own particular brand of havoc in there. And when the work was more or less completed, the controversial subject of this conversation, died.

So we shall never know.

R.I.P Tony.

What goes around . . .

A while ago, I saw my brother cry.
Old then, gone now - but before . . .
Big, happy, long distance Biker -
Reduced to tears.

He was unpacking gifts.
What's up, I said.
He looked at me sadly.
I didn't get anything, he said, trying not to sob.
Oh come on. It looks a pretty good haul to me, I said,
peeved.

No, no, I mean I didn't BRING anything.
I can't get out much, see?
Look Love, it's fine . . .
Placating - not comprehending.
He had a charming smile.

The years have gone and it's today.
I view it all - the paper, the packing, the drinks
from my chair.
I put small cheques
into sterile white envelopes.
And now I get it . . . I understand.

I can't get out much, see?
And my smile is domino dots.

2011

So there I am, all unsuspecting, left with a delightful little unit and nowhere to go. 'You can sell it now, if you like,' said the Building Inspector on his final inspection. 'All done - all complies and very nice too.' I was completely shattered. 'SELL IT,' I choked on the words. 'Not likely - no, not at all, but thank you.' 'Oh Right Ho,' he said cheerfully and departed.

Picking myself up, recovering from such sacrilege I departed too, to the other side of the new wall. Sell it . . . I don't think so. No. Never. But, you see, I believe the Judge and the house had a hand in all of this.

The Piper had to be paid.

That was all going on in about 1993. I am writing this in 2012, so much of the rancour, the regret, the heartbreak . . . has finally gone. And we still have the Chapel.

One day, sometime later, I was relating all this to a young friend called Nicola. Licking my wounds a bit, I suppose, and going on about how strange and unfair life could be. Nic was in Antiques too and as we chatted we cleaned and spat on bits of brass and silver we had just bought. She heard about the brother who had died somewhat inconveniently and she heard about the turbulent Priest, whom had been summarily dismissed after a long legal battle. His linen was well washed and hung out to dry and I was finally rid . . . only to find he had to be paid a vast sum of money. Words failed me then. Words fail me now so we won't go there again.

'The Law is made by man, for man,' said lovely solicitor, weeping into his dollar-printed gauze. 'Nothing is fair,' he said. 'This is the Law we are talking about - not Justice.' Yeah right. Well that was certainly true. It may be different now. I hope so.

So there I am, with this delightful little unit, no brother, plans gone to pot as they so often do and a vast great sum of money to find.

'Sell it,' said Nic. 'Could you sell it?' I replied that no, I really didn't think I could diminish the house I had sweated blood to keep. It would be a travesty of all I felt and believed and no, I couldn't bear to leave it. Not after all that.

'Then let it,' she said. 'We'll have it. Si and I will have it.'

And they did.

Nicola (Nic) Simon and their 2 children are all in Australia now - Go well

And there started a long trail of really nice people who have lived in and loved the Chapel over many years. Some for short periods between houses, some between jobs, but all have loved it . . . have loved being there . . . have loved being part of the set up. They have kept the wolf from my door. And the Judge and the house have watched over all. We have kept the faith.

And we still have the Chapel, the early bit, the original bit which dwells quietly to the east.

Nicola . . . on leaving Chapel Cottage

1st October 2004

Her eyes are sad now.
With everything to smile about
she's sad.
She has her sea lord standing tall
who loves her . . .
and yet . . .

Her eyes are sad now
in spite of being beautiful
she's sad.
She has this sense of fun
and everyone's afraid of her
and yet . . .

Her eyes are sad now
even though she's quicksilver
she's sad.
So sensitive and talented
and everybody loves her
and yet . . .

Her eyes are sad now
with everything before her
and much already learned -
so funny, witty, wise beyond her years.
She has it all
and yet . . .

Her eyes are happier now, although
compassion is an obstacle.
She takes his hand and slowly walks away.
But looking back . . .
covertly she flicks away a tear.
'I loved that little house,' she said,
'we were so happy here.'

The Girl in the woods

Where the trees are tall - and the grass is smooth -
And the daisies nudge the sun -
She dwells . . .

She is the laughter in the shimmering Birch -
The chattering in the Holly -
The welcome in the Rose.

She has the grace of the Lime -
The compassion of the Willow -
And the humour of the Olive.

She will march with the Bamboo -
Stand firm with the Beech -
And endure with the Mulberry.

Outrageous as the Sycamore -
Colourful as the Sumac -
And wise as the Gingko.

Open handed as the Ash -
Charming as the Prunus -
She is the smile in the bowing Yew.

But the innate knowledge of Good -
The firmness of Spirit and the strength of Purpose -
The epitome of Time -
Is the gift of the Oak - the mighty Oak -
The Mighty English Oak.

Where the trees are tall - and the grass is smooth -
And the daisies nudge the sun -
She dwells . . .

For Amanda, who is of course, the Girl in the Woods

27th January 2012

Part XIII

Into each Life . . .

'Life is what happens to you while you're busy making other plans'

How true. And how could the late, great, John Lennon have known that sadly it would have been almost as appropriate had he said 'death' and not 'life,' for he was gunned down close to his home in 1980. He was 40 years of age. What a waste. We shall never know of his being and becoming, which would surely have been such an interesting developing of a talented life.

So yes, I became a huge Beatles fan, along with the rest of the world, and thought it quite part of my daughter's education, then aged about 10, to be dragged to the village hall, to watch 'Help' and or 'A Hard day's Night' on a splintery screen and with terrible acoustics. I don't believe she complained too much and in fact in the '90s, her own daughter, then just a tot, would sit strapped into her car seat, singing all the Beatles tracks, which she knew word for word and she still does.

'She gotta ticketa ri-hi-hide an she donekerr.'

Nothing wrong with that and howzatt for constancy.

I have a book containing the Beatles' lyrics from 1962 - 1970, their early work. No music, just the words - and I tell you, that - is - poetry . . .'waits at the window, wearing a face that she keeps in a jar by the door' . . . and . . . 'Pools of sorrow, waves of joy are drifting through my open mind, possessing and caressing me . . .' . . . 'Thoughts meander like a restless wind and tumble blindly as they make their way across the Universe . . .' Can you do that? I can't. And read - READ - The Long and Winding Road . . . Is that a prayer, or what?

And speaking of his untimely death, there is a Lennon quote . . . 'I don't intend to be a performing flea anymore. I was the dreamweaver, but although I'll be running at 20,000 miles an hour trying to prove myself, I don't want to die at 40.'

Was that prophetic? I leave you with that thought.

The Long and Winding Road

The long and winding road that leads to your door,
will never disappear, I've seen that road before
it always leads me here, leads me to your door.

The wild and windy night that the rain washed away,
has left a pool of tears crying for the day.
Why leave me standing here, let me know the way.

Many times I've been alone, many times I've cried,
Anyway you'll never know the many ways I've tried,
But still they lead me back to the long and winding road.

You left me standing here a long, long time ago.
Don't leave me waiting here,
Oh, lead me to your door.

Lennon & McCartney 1969

It is a matter of some difficulty to work out whether this is a prayer, a meditation or just a kid grappling with the growing pains of love. No doubt it is all of these things, but the words say so much.

And this seems the right time to think about TOM. Tom was Matthew's friend and Matt is my nephew. Tom has absolutely nothing to do with John Lennon, or so it would seem. In fact Tom was not even born before John died in 1980. Of course, like the rest of the world, Tom would have known of John as an Icon. The first thing they have in common is that they were much loved people.

Matthew came to see me one spring morning and I have to say he looked phased. And over a cup of coffee he said simply, 'My friend Tom was found dead on Sunday. He killed himself.' Clearly in shock, Matt went on, 'I don't know why, nobody does. It's been awful and think of his parents.' I was of course doing just that, my head was spinning and you can't help thinking of your own kids.

Pale but without tears, he continued . . . 'Why would he do that? Why would anyone do that? On Thursday, we were out in his car. He had fitted some smart new lights and we drove out to show them off. On Thursday he was alive and happy. And today he's dead. He was 19. We, his friends just can't believe it.'

Matt was devastated and there was nothing really that I could do to help him.

Tom

Well, you've done it this time
secret, silent unrehearsed - in shock,
we are your pale-faced friends, who loved you
And quietly, you simply walked away.
Now you are our focus.

Ants scurrying demented around confusing whichway
scrabbling the eggs of our future
desperately trying to preserve
the footsteps you have left in the sand,
knowing their impermanence.
And all because you lifted our stone.

Yesterday we were young, giggling in the restroom,
preening in the mirror above the basin,
time for one more drag - Top chicks.
And close by - giving scant consideration
to the Middle East - which doesn't affect us -
more to the rugby - which does -
bragging butch about the bird we'll pull tonight
We were all just kids.

Today we are all so old -
catapulted unprepared, into a world we do not know
and cannot handle.
Help us, Tom,
to deal with emotions we do not understand . . .
to face your Mum and Dad, who made you,
fashioned you from their love -
to grapple with your space left empty -
to soften the thoughts we cannot bear -
Your last terrible moments alone
and the burning rope.

We need to know,
standing under the canopy of the stars
and looking up,
white faces smudged bruise black,
that your spirit is free
and gliding above all of this,
that you are finally at peace . . .
We need to forgive.

Imagine

Imagine there's no heaven
It's easy if you try
No hell below us
Above us only sky
Imagine all the people
Living for today . . .
Imagine there's no countries
It isn't hard to do
Nothing to kill or die for
And no religion too
Imagine all the people
Living life in peace . . .
You may say I'm a dreamer
But I'm not the only one
I hope someday you'll join us
And the world will be as one
Imagine no possessions
I wonder if you can
No need for greed or hunger
A brotherhood of man
Imagine all the people
Sharing all the world . . .
You may say I'm a dreamer
But I'm not the only one
I hope someday you'll join us
And the world will live as one

John Lennon 1971

Christine Turner

I have to write this down before I forget, before the facts get twisted, before the whole episode drops into the obscurity, which subsequent unimportant and unrelated everyday events inevitably bring . . . and before I start fussing like Martha.

I have never met Christine, Chris, but I feel I know her very well through her son, Kevin, of whom I wrote a while ago since he has a fantastic story. However, that was then and this is now and this is quite another story.

Kevin is my Physio. He speaks perfunctorily of his garden, his work, the book he is, or is not, reading, of the frustration of the property market and occasionally, his family. He has to keep rabbiting on, (and I do my fair share,) to disguise my yelps of pain as he works on my back. Recently, he had been increasingly concerned about his mother's health. Just a couple of weeks ago I asked his mother's name. 'Christine,' he said, 'Chris'.

He didn't ask why I asked and I didn't tell him. There was no need. And my reason, of course, had been Prayer. Don't get me wrong - I am an extremely limping Christian, but my Faith is strong and I do believe in the power of prayer.

As I held Christine up that night, basically asking for guidance and pain relief for her, what came insistently to me was 'God Knows' - the poem written by Minnie Louise Haskins and which everyone knows as 'The Gate of the Year.' This was one of Queen Elizabeth, the Queen Mother's favourite pieces . . . and which King George VI recited in his Christmas Speech in 1939.

Over and over I said this piece - time and time again - until gradually I felt its calm and perhaps some peace for Chris. I cannot know that but I hoped it might be so.

Yesterday Kevin was distraught, though covering well, like the trouper he is. His mother's condition had markedly deteriorated. There seemed little hope of recovery.

With not much hesitation I gave him the piece . . . Gate of the Year. He quickly read it, nodding in recognition as he did so and I suggested he might give it to her . . . or not. What a cheek to intrude in this way.

But in that moment we silently cried together - each without the other's knowledge. Perhaps it helped him a bit. Who knows? God Knows.

And that evening I suffered the agonies of the damned. I should not have given him that poem. I should certainly not have suggested he gave it to his mother. It was pushing the boundaries of professional friendship too far. And it was a dreadful cheek.

Later, much later, too late, I text my apology for introducing the God slot and received a charming reply. His mother, who had refused treatment thus far, had been taken into hospital where she was 'on drip, morphine and god knows what (with a small G) and at last some pain control.' Kevin and his young wife were so relieved and actually thanked me for my input. I of course, had done nothing. But I had prayed and would continue to do so. And that should have been the end of it. But it was not. Sleep came reluctantly, but eventually I fell into a fitful drowse. A drowse . . . not a sleep.

And someone was there, in the room, with me. Oh look, do go away, please. I am completely shattered. It was Christine . . . I did not see her. I did not need to. But she was there and she was hungry. How did I know that? I knew.

There was only one answer - I had to go down and get her something to eat. Oh No. So off I went, grumbling a bit. Dressing gown and all. And when you say I was sleep walking - I was not. I don't do sleep walking - I barely sleep . . . also I do have to be very careful on stairs and hang on to the banister rail.

I clearly remember switching on lights, being careful on the stairs, crossing the hall and unlocking the kitchen door.

I made a whopping great navvy cheese sandwich - cut it in halves - and put each on a plate. And these two plates I carried back upstairs . . . and Christine had gone. Gone. Well thank you very much, Chris.

But she had gone away happy. How can you know that? You cannot possibly know she went away happy. You cannot even know she was there. Oh yes, she was there and she went away happy. I know.

And I had God on my side, so there.

So I am happy too. I have been happy ever since.

Christine is all right. She is accepting and relieved and loved. After all, she hadn't had to make the decision. She believes in Fate. And she has God on her side, whether or not she knows it. I ate my bit of the huge sandwich. War babies can't waste anything. Her bit was on its plate on the bedside table when I woke up after the best sleep, ever. It's in the freezer. The birds can have it. But I'll keep it for the moment to remind me. To remind me that Christine is content.

She knows she is loved.

' . . . and put your hand into the hand of God,

That shall be better to you than light,

And safer than a known way . . .'

Rest peacefully Christine – 30th September 2012

Everybody Hurts

When your day is long
And the night, the night is yours alone
When you're sure you've had enough
Of this life, well hang on

Don't let yourself go
'Cause everybody cries
And everybody hurts sometimes

Sometimes everything is wrong
Now it's time to sing along
When your day is night alone (Hold on, hold on)
If you feel like letting go (Hold on)
If you think you've had too much
Of this life, well hang on

Everybody hurts
Take comfort in your friends
Everybody hurts
Don't throw your hand, oh no

Don't throw your hand
If you feel like you're alone
No, no, no, you are not alone

If you're on your own in this life
The days and nights are long
When you think you've had too much of this life to hang on

Well, everybody hurts sometimes
Everybody cries
Everybody hurts sometimes
And everybody hurts sometimes
So hold on, hold on
Hold on, hold on, hold on, hold on, hold on, hold on
Everybody hurts

R.E.M 1992

And in the midst of all of that we had the Olympics . . .

And from a long list of applicants, they selected Kevin. Well they would, wouldn't they, given his history.

He of course, said he would have to decline. His mother dared him to do so. In fact she 'instructed' him to accept and to get on and do it - and to enjoy it.

HANDS ON HELPER:
Physio Kevin Turner
volunteered at the
sailing academy

PHYSIOTHERAPIST Kevin Turner of Bridport hailed the success of the Olympics after a hands-on experience at Portland.

He gave expert care to competitors at the sailing academy as they faced some of the biggest races of their lives.

Kevin, of West Street, was picked to work at the academy after a gruelling interview and selection process.

He said that the pressure was huge but that every single athlete and co-worker was a pleasure to work with.

"Over the course of my two weeks I treated everything from pre-event massage to dislocated shoulders, sprained ankles to whiplash necks, sailors bringing up the rear of their field in their very first Olympics to gold medallists.

"Almost every sporting injury came through the clinic as well as athletes wanting a final check over before their event."

He added: "Highlights of my time were meeting Ben Ainslie and a handshake from the Duke of Edinburgh.

"The whole experience was one to remember.

"Although people tend to think of a physio as only treating or preventing injuries, these Olympics were the ideal platform to show how a physio can improve not only sporting performance but also how improving human movement can enhance the general wellbeing of the population."

Bridport and Lyme Regis News Wednesday August 15th 2012

Let it Be

When I find myself in times of trouble
Mother Mary comes to me . . .
Speaking words of wisdom, let it be.
And in my hour of darkness
She is standing right in front of me
Speaking words of wisdom, let it be.
Let it be . . . Let it be.
Whisper words of wisdom, let it be.

And when the broken hearted people
Living in the world agree,
There will be an answer, let it be.
For though they may be parted there is
Still a chance that they may see
There will be an answer, let it be.
Let it be . . . Let it be.
There will be an answer, let it be

And when the night is cloudy,
There is still a light that shines on me,
Shine until tomorrow, let it be.
I wake up to the sound of music,
Mother Mary comes to me,
Speaking words of wisdom, let it be.
Let it be, let it be.
There will be an answer, let it be.

Let it be . . . Let it be,
Whisper words of wisdom, let it be.

Lennon & McCartney 1969

He Ain't Heavy

The road is long
With many a winding turn
That leads us to who knows where
Who knows when
But I'm strong
Strong enough to carry him
He ain't heavy, he's my brother

So on we go
His welfare is of my concern
No burden is he to bear
We'll get there
For I know
He would not encumber me
He ain't heavy, he's my brother

If I'm laden at all
I'm laden with sadness
That everyone's heart
Isn't filled with the gladness
Of love for one another

It's a long, long road
From which there is no return
While we're on the way to there
Why not share
And the load
Doesn't weigh me down at all
He ain't heavy, he's my brother

He's my brother
He ain't heavy, he's my brother . . .

The Hollies 1970

All shall be well
And all shall be well
And all manner of things
Shall be well

Dame Julian of Norwich   14th Century mystic

244

Part XIV

Nearing the end!

Going Back . . .

You can't go back . . . Not really . . . Not after all those years . . . And anyway, there is only ever a 50% chance of things turning out as you hope. Mostly they don't.

And what we wanted to do was so simple.

We just wanted to show the girls the Forest . . . and Belmont. So on the way back from Dorset to London, we turned right at Cadnam Roundabout. It is a lovely route, the trees part just enough to allow the road to wind through and Lyndhurst is only a few miles east.

The first bit of deja vu along there is the leafy and overgrown entrance to the wartime home of Oakmount School, where I did my first stint of pupil teaching - I was the pupil. I was seventeen. And my teacher, Jamie, became a lifelong friend. We were both so young. But not to confuse the issue . . . leave that for another time.

Coming into Lyndhurst, we turned left and went round the one way circuit. So short the circuit - so long ago and so many the events and memories. For instance, half way round on the junction with the road to Brockenhurst, in a house romantically called Beechings Over, there dwelt a girl, one time bridesmaid, Anne. Still there . . . you have to wonder . . . who knows?

And you can't go back . . . not really . . . not after all those years . . .

And then we came to Granville at Gascoines. Only we didn't. Gascoines, a huge and beautiful country house, set in acres of gardens and land and hidden behind the church, was the war time home of Granville College, when the constant bombing of Southampton became too hot and worried parents threatened to remove their girls.

'That was the fifth Form' - 'That window there' - 'Which window where?'

Oh no, it was all different - everything was changed. It looked like twenty five thousand flats, higgledy piggledy, all over the place. Oh no.

After all, that's your childhood - your childhood ghosts - the tears and the tennis - swept away. All those girls - doing their Prep.

You can't go back . . . not really . . . not after all those years.

We'll go on then. Another couple of miles and we will see the Forest. That'll be the same. The Forest won't have changed. We'll show them the special bit . . . the bit beyond Keepers Cottage and into the wonderful woods.

The tall trees, the scrubland, the nests and the brambles.

And we will listen to the silence.

It will be as it always was . . . forests don't change. Along the worn path with all those ant hills - one - two - three . . . more - where in a seething mass of needles, pine needles laboriously gathered, year on year, centuries of ants dwelt - where we pushed a bit of stick in . . . and fled. On up the worn path with woodland birds shouting. Past the murky pond - that was bottomless, you understand, filled with reeds that liked it . . . no fish nor frogs, that didn't. On, on, up the worn path, to where it all changed . . . and we would be in the Cathedral. The girls would like this bit. Less dense now, light and open, sunshine glinting through majestic Beech trees, hundreds of them - and always, the quiet, the silence. This is where we looked for the Giant . . . Quite scary.

The ground here was soft and brown - thick, thick with loam, cosseted and warmed by layers of bronze leaves - which we scuffed and kicked into a shower, diving in, shouting and laughing. Where a few years later, the girl and the young swain sat on a bank and swirled their feet, not into the sea, but into the layers of crunchy, dry, brown leaves . . . gathering them into a shower around them. That was the day the man appeared behind them - just appeared, standing there.

'Get up slowly and walk away . . . slowly,' the young swain said, 'walk away and don't look back,' which they did, holding hands, a bit scared. The girl did - look back that is - and the man was nowhere to be seen. But he had been there, they had both seen him.

Perhaps he came to wish them well. They got married, from Belmont, soon after that, the girl and the young swain. We'll find that bank. The girls would like that. It's odd looking back . . .

Anyway, on to the bridge over the railway, with Lyndhurst Road station down there - or is it - now turn right and then left and there is the cricket pitch. The square where the fathers played the game and the mothers made the tea. Keep going along the gravelly track and we'll come to the Keepers Cottage. It's just along there.

Excited now, going back - with the girls. Unfortunately, it didn't work out. For there in front, right across the track was a huge gate with an equally huge fence at either side. Our way was entirely blocked.

A couple of youngsters arrived on bikes, which they threw over the horrible gate, walked through a kissing gate and went on their way. They had done it all before and were not the slightest bit interested in us - why would they be. We were just another lot of trippers, come to gawp. We were utterly non plussed. How could this be happening?

The New Forest is an Ancient Heritage site - you can't just sling a vast great gate and fence across the track and get away with it, can you? Clearly you can. Clearly they can. Wouldn't do in my day - nor my Dad's. We'd have waved flags. Sat down. Complained. Shouted. So what to do? Oh damn.

It seems that the answer to everything is Ice Cream and by sheer fluke we just happened to be at the rear of The Angry Cheese Hotel and there was a garden gate. I was angry all right . . . but nothing daunted, the girls went off and came back with a selection. They had no idea what they were missing - and food is food for all that. I minded so much and the old Volvo snorted in disgust - and in reverse.

You can't go back . . . not really . . . not after all those years.

Recovering a bit and keeping up appearances, me not them . . . oh how could these little townies know . . . we'll go on then. I'll show them Belmont - where I grew up, in spite of the war.

Another few hundred yards - STOP - on the left, just here, stop. It's the one on the right. Oh NO.

Belmont was one of a pair of turn of the century detached villas, with a Tudor palaver sort of edge to them. Never mind. Belmont had a huge garden, good for Digging for Victory, a large garage, where the brother constantly took one of his bikes to bits - and never got the putting back together quite right - and a big piece of extra land called Nomansland. Great fun.

Don't cry - don't cry - think of the children.

Oh, but what changes. What terribleness. What - why - when - how could they? For what reason? Money I suppose.

The drive with the arches - gone. The lawns - gone. The garage - gone. The lawn was a car park. Nomansland had three houses on it - three houses - and the Garage was a house. A fully fledged house. Three up and three down probably. And everything was white. White big house - Tudor palaver gone - fair enough. White small house. All white, everything white, shouting, Look at me, ha! Look at me, ha! I don't like it, which is quite all right, because it's not your house any more. But look. No gate . . . But the huge Oak is still there. And you don't live there any more. Right Ho. Thank the Lord for that.

The daughter did offer kindly, seeing I was marginally upset, to knock and ask if we could go in and have a look . . . which kindness was declined, pronto, with thanks.

I did take a scant look through almost closed fingertips, at Sturminster, the other half of the unassuming pair. Oh, Praise Be. Sturminster was just the same. Sturminster had not changed - Sturminster still had its bit of Tudor palaver. I almost liked it. Tired and a bit faded, the front garden not quite so loved, but who cares. Sturminster lives on. The years fell away. We were all kids again. Climbing the knotty trees in their orchard, even though scrumping was always so much more fun. Oh. One thing - that one precious thing remained the same. Thank you God.

We'd better get on. Long way to go. Stuff to do. We'll get something to eat on the way. But I'll tell you something, it's probably difficult going back. You might get a really bad shock - or of course it may be a great experience.

Your call. Your choice. Your spin.

But you can't go back . . . not really . . . not after all those tears. Q.E.D.

Seebackoscope

Well, I've just read all that through . . . and what a shock that was. Absolutely nothing like I foresaw, at all. I have heard proper writers say that they are never quite sure where their characters will take them. Now I understand. This compilation is nothing, but nothing, as I envisaged. It was meant simply to be host to my poetry and general pieces . . . just a little poem or series, joined by a daisy chain of cotton wool clouds of connective tissue. And what have we ended up with? Well, it's a kind of biography or autobiography, a seventy year waltz through the woods of the 20th Century . . . I am quite surprised at myself and with it.

If I were going to rant on about the war, then why not do it properly? Southampton was not always a burnt out wreck; it had been a beautiful tree lined city, its old University buildings dominating; a long established place of learning. It is strange that the 1930 Civic Centre, with its Clock Tower and its green a la mode tiles survived the Blitz . . . and still stands proud today. The one thing the oldies thought could well have gone.

Why no mention of the Bargate? 'Above and Below Bar' was an important logistical point, an ancient part of the city wall . . . Above Bar the parks, shops and theatres, Below Bar the Port.

Why no mention of the beautiful liners, which we saw as they lay in the dry dock, as we travelled by bus between city and forest? We read their names and have now forgotten, names writ large. I do remember the Lusitania and of course the maiden voyage of the great Queen Mary, with her three funnels. I watched as she came up Southampton Water, coming home. I wonder if they heard our clapping?

Then all this ranting about the war, my bit of the war. Why not research it properly, instead of picking out random bits of it? And whatever happened to the Gulf war which, although it was later, had me sitting on the edge of my seat and listening to the world service all night. I suppose it brought it all back, hearing the shells and bombs and the graphic reports and descriptions. Listening in a dark room.

But the war, horrible as it was, taught me a great deal and it taught me to listen to my father, not that he would ever speak of his experiences in the Great War, while he was serving with the Coldstreams. They never will, will they? But he was a wise man.

So that fluffy daisy chain of little events, to join the poems, rather went by the board. And of course it has ended up as something of a hymn to The Beatles.

Nothing wrong with that. They do it so much better than I.

Olive Betty Tony Rena

So, that is probably more than enough. I should stop now. Although . . .
Still poems not included . . .
Still items not covered . . .
All the gardens . . . All the trees . . .
All the animals who have been such a large part of life . . .
And of course, the seagulls . . . that life-long, on-off, love-hate relationship
But actually, on a work like this, where do you stop - when really,
nothing has been covered adequately or in depth?
And really, if anyone, apart from the press ganged, has got this far, it is
only fair to let them off the hook . . .

Except . . .

Tappie   Mrs Tappie   Tappette

The Waiting Game

The Gulls glide, calling
And Jacks swoop and chatter.
The Robin waits, quiet
And the fat Thrush listens.
The Blackbird marches, pert
And the Sparrow tweets, busy.
Jenny wren, soprano sweet
Softly brown - here, there, gone . . .
And now we wait . . .

Spring 2012

Anya growing

The light was dim and nearly gone,
The corridor was long, so long,
The carpet soft was blue, so blue
The frightened nurse was new, so new.
Her name was Anya.

Slowly she walked from door to door,
Listening and peering that all was well,
Playing over the consoles there
and touching the flowers upon them
Unreal, of course.

At No.14 she stopped alert . . .
She heard it again, a chuckle,
In Poland the word was not the same,
The sound the same,
A chuckle.

The one within could neither speak,
nor see, nor hear, nor move . . .
nor recognise the day.
But clearly,
she could chuckle.

The young one went upon her way,
Listening and peering that all was well,
No longer frightened, no longer new,
A smiling Anya.

Her work complete, softly returned,
Silently in at No.14
Quiet she dropped on the carpet blue
and there she stayed, the whole night through
hugging her knees, and dreaming.
A loving Anya.

She saw the old one young again,
Swaying and spinning in gown of blue
and small satin slippers
with funny heels,

And distinctly, heard the chuckle.
As night turned softly into day
and darkness into light,
These two inert, in Peace they slept . . .
Just one of them, still breathing.

Anya, grown up, no longer new,
Went on with all she had to do
Confident and full of Grace . . .
And Love, is Universal.

I Chuckle . . . therefore I am . . .

For Freddie and Amanda Addo

The Red Queen

Here the Red Queen, clip - clopping,

hooped skirt swinging,

thrusts high on the air

a myriad shining lights

weaving and soaring above and around,

spilling orbs of dazzling joy,

to settle around you.

A lapful of moments, carved in time.

All is changed . . . All is the same . . .

All is well.

The Hotel Alexandra - Lyme Regis

Stable, in a changing world,
The Alexandra's flag unfurled,
A welcome harbinger of glee,
For me and for my good friend Dee,
With cauliflower florets.

We run the gauntlet of the hill -
Come early - so there're places still -
Step nimbly in, across the cobble,
On four inch heels that make us wobble -
For cauliflower florets.

Breathless, we attain the venue,
Languidly reach for the menu,
Spritzer over ice for Dee,
Dry Martini's fine for me -
With cauliflower florets.

But what is this - it cannot be,
It couldn't happen - not to Dee -
The world comes crashing round our ears,
We've realized our darkest fears -
No cauliflower florets.

The Management could do no more,
With us recumbent on the floor,
Than fan us with a menu handy
And pour us both a double Brandy -
lieu of cauliflower florets.

We did not want the Channel Tunnel,
Far rather go by air or funnel,
We did not vote the EEC -
Not anyone, not even Dee,
Just cauliflower florets.

We did not fight them on the Beaches,
Allow with ease the Hordes to reach us,
And alter now our Bill of Fare -
Blue pencil here without a care
Our cauliflower florets.

Upon a Thursday - deep in the vault,
A Spirit moves - it's all your fault,
A sylvan spectre gliding through -
Five thousand liege men, good and true
Crying, 'Cauliflower Florets'.

Old Alexandra, stately still,
Articulates this bitter pill -
'These things - they are an institution,
Writ large in British Constitution -
These cauliflower florets'

'Consider now, though Chef may hate it,
I order that you reinstate it -
Or I shall nightly walk these portals
And terrify your timid mortals,
Wailing . . . Cauliflower Florets'.

'And furthermore,' in Queenly haut,
'there's less on menu to be bought . . .
Strategy better in my day -
Just fill 'em up, and make 'em pay -
Increase the price by fifty pence,
A winner . . . here is evidence -
These Cauliflower Florets'!

The Listeners

'Is there anybody there?' said the Traveller,
Knocking on the moonlit door;
And his horse in the silence champed the grass
Of the forest's ferny floor;
And a bird flew up out of the turret,
Above the Traveller's head:
And he smote upon the door again a second time;
'Is there anybody there?' he said.
But no one descended to the Traveller
No head from the leaf-fringed sill
Leaned over and looked into his grey eyes,
Where he stood perplexed and still.
But only a host of phantom listeners
That dwelt in the lone house then
Stood listening in the quiet of the moonlight
To that voice from the world of men:
Stood thronging the faint moonbeams on the dark stair,
That goes down to the empty hall,
Hearkening in an air stirred and shaken
By the lonely Traveller's call.
And he felt in his heart their strangeness,
Their stillness answering his cry,
While his horse moved, cropping the dark turf,
'Neath the starred and leafy sky;
For he suddenly smote on the door, even
Louder, and lifted his head
'Tell them I came, and no one answered,
That I kept my word,' he said.
Never the least stir made the listeners,
Though every word he spake
Fell echoing through the shadowiness of the still house
From the one man left awake:
Ay, they heard his foot upon the stirrup,
And the sound of iron on stone,
And how the silence surged softly backward,
When the plunging hoofs were gone.

Walter de la Mare - written 1912

Home . . .

Home is where you want to be -
Where you feel content -
Most of the time, anyway -
Where in any case, you feel completely secure -
And you know exactly where you are -
Exactly.

Home is you, it is what you have made it.
It is how you want it to be -
The sofas get more faded -
But you know exactly where they are -
Without looking.

The photos on the mantelpiece stay the same -
While the people within are older -
They groan and complain and say change them -
The clock in the middle seldom says the right time -
You like it all, just as it is.

There's dust behind the curtains -
The books on the table stay the same -
And the footstool slightly awry,
Oh but, the flowers, the flowers in the corner -
Are always fresh.

People come, invited of course -
They are just as slow as you -
You've known each other for years,
You stagger round - the pain will go -
Let's have a drink.

Now that, is something we can do
With long years of practice -
We know what we like, no problem.
So yes, actually, we can all hold a glass,
Easily - and with aplomb.

And so here I live . . .
Coexisting with those
who have gone before.
The unlikely smell of
pipe tobacco in the hall.
The knowledge of the little serving girl,
dressed in early costume looking down.
The occasional chattering in the aura . . .
And the love.

Always the love.

All You Need is LOVE

Love - love - love, Love - love - love, Love - love - love . . .
There's nothing you can do that can't be done,
Nothing you can sing that can't be sung,
Nothing you can say but you can learn how to play the game . . .
It's easy.
There' s nothing you can make that can't be made,
No one you can save that can't be saved,
Nothing you can do but you can learn how to be in time . . .
It's easy.
All you need is love - All you need is love -
All you need is love, love - Love is all you need.
Nothing you can see that isn't shown . . .
Nowhere you can be that isn't where you're meant to be . . .
It's easy.

All you need is love - all you need is love.
All you need is love, love . . .
Love is all you need.

Lennon & McCartney 1967

And was it all worth it?

Well of course it was, I'm still here aren't I - well and happy and old. And time, the years and well life really, has simply flown on the wind.

As it does.

And so I sit here, in beautiful Dorset - hermitoid and happy - sans teeth, sans eyes, sans taste, sans everything . . . hiding in the home and garden I love, and doing my very best to fend off all comers. So far, a long life, lived fully. Nothing has been easy - everything worthwhile.

You don't stop being young because you grow old - you grow old because you stop being young . . .

And it ain't over yet!

Bridge over Troubled Water

When you're weary
Feeling small
When tears are in your eyes
I will dry them all
I'm on your side
When times get rough
And friends just can't be found
Like a bridge over troubled water
I will lay me down
Like a bridge over troubled water
I will lay me down

When you're down and out
When you're on the street
When evening falls so hard
I will comfort you
I'll take your part
When darkness comes
And pain is all around
Like a bridge over troubled water
I will lay me down
Like a bridge over troubled water
I will lay me down

Sail on Silver Girl,
Sail on by
Your time has come to shine
All your dreams are on their way
See how they shine
If you need a friend
I'm sailing right behind
Like a bridge over troubled water
I will ease your mind
Like a bridge over troubled water
I will ease your mind

Simon and Garfunkel 1969

Remember me . . .

Remember me when I am gone away,
Gone far away into the silent land;
When you can no more hold me by the hand,
Nor I half turn to go yet turning stay.
Remember me when no more day by day
You tell me of our future that you planned:
Only remember me; you understand
It will be late to counsel then or pray.
Yet if you should forget me for a while
And afterwards remember, do not grieve:
For if the darkness and corruption leave
A vestige of the thoughts that once I had,
Better by far you should forget and smile
Than that you should remember and be sad

Christina Rossetti

Life is what happens to you while you're busy making other plans.

Appendix

* * *

Photographs and Original Images:

p. 55 Shutterstock image (766645291) 'Waves crashing against a dock' by Matteo Porru

p. 97, 99 and 101 Classic Jaguars. Original water colours by Eldieter instagram.com/@eldieter

p.238 Original watercolour of John Lennon by Roberto Erre instagram.com/@erre.art

p. 264 Woodland by Diane Hinson instagram.com/@experiments_in_the_attic

Of course I would like to use Lennon's quote again . . . and again . . . but that is his and not mine – so to round things off, when I find life happening to me while I'm busy making other plans, I tell myself to 'get a grip and just do it.'

Jane

All You Need is Love

Printed in Great Britain
by Amazon